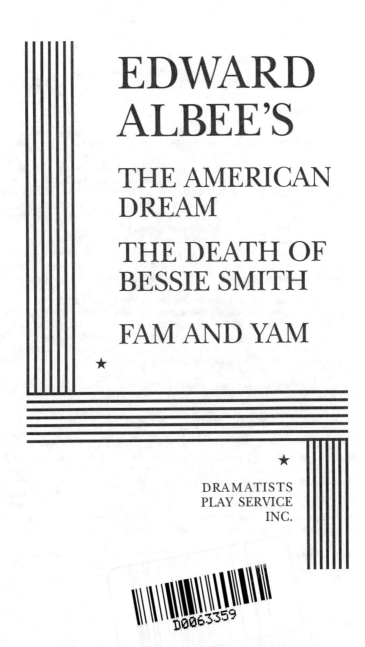

# EDWARD ALBEE'S

## THE AMERICAN DREAM

## THE DEATH OF BESSIE SMITH

## FAM AND YAM

★

DRAMATISTS
PLAY SERVICE
INC.

# The American Dream

## (1959-1960)

FOR DAVID DIAMOND

THE AMERICAN DREAM was first produced by Theatre 1961, Richard Barr and Clinton Wilder, at the York Playhouse, New York City, on January 24, 1961. It was directed by Alan Schneider. The sets and costumes were by William Ritman. The cast was as follows:

DADDY .........................................John C. Becher

MOMMY ........................................Jane Hoffman

GRANDMA .........................................Sudie Bond

MRS. BARKER ................................Nancy Cushman

THE YOUNG MAN ...................................Ben Piazza

# The American Dream

*A living room. Two armchairs, one toward either side of the stage, facing each other diagonally out toward the audience. Against the rear wall, a sofa. A door, leading out from the apartment, in the rear wall, far R., an archway, leading to other rooms, in the side wall, L. At the beginning, Daddy is seated in the armchair L. Curtain up. A silence, then—Mommy enters from L.*

MOMMY. (*Crossing to R. arch.*) I don't know what can be keeping them.

DADDY. They're late, naturally.

MOMMY. Of course, they're late; it never fails.

DADDY. That's the way things are today, and there's nothing you can do about it.

MOMMY. You're quite right. (*Sits chair R.*)

DADDY. When we took this apartment, they were quick enough to have me sign the lease; they were quick enough to take my check for two months rent in advance . . .

MOMMY. . . . and one month's security . . .

DADDY. . . . and one month's security. They were quick enough to check my references; they were quick enough about all that. But now! But now, try to get the ice-box fixed, try to get the door bell fixed, try to get the leak in the johnny fixed! Just try it . . . they aren't so quick about *that*.

MOMMY. Of course not; it never fails. People think they can get away with anything these days . . . and, of course they can. I went to buy a new hat yesterday. (*Pause.*) I said, I went to buy a new hat yesterday.

DADDY. Oh! Yes . . . yes.

MOMMY. Pay attention.

DADDY. I *am* paying attention, Mommy.

MOMMY. Well, be sure you do.

DADDY. Oh, I am.

MOMMY. All right, Daddy; now listen.

DADDY. I'm listening, Mommy.

MOMMY. You're sure!

DADDY. Yes . . . yes, I'm sure. I'm all ears.

MOMMY. (*Giggles at the thought, then.*) All right, now. I went to buy a new hat yesterday and I said, "I'd like a new hat, please." And so, they showed me a few hats, green ones and blue ones, and I didn't like any of them, not one bit. What did I say? What did I just say?

DADDY. You didn't like any of them, not one bit.

MOMMY. That's right; you just keep paying attention. And then they showed me one that I did like. It was a lovely little hat, and I said, "Oh, this is a lovely little hat; I'll take this hat, oh my, it's lovely. What color is it?" And they said, "Why this is beige; isn't it a lovely little beige hat?" And I said, "Oh, it's just lovely." And so, I bought it. (*Stops, looks at Daddy.*)

DADDY. (*To show he is paying attention.*) And so you bought it.

MOMMY. And so I bought it, and I walked out of the store with the hat right on my head, and I ran spang into the chairman of our women's club, and she said, "Oh, my dear, isn't that a lovely little hat? Where did you get that lovely little hat? It's the loveliest little hat; I've always wanted a wheat-colored hat *myself*." And I said, "Why, no, my dear; this hat is beige; beige." And she laughed, and said, "Why no my dear, that's a wheat colored hat; wheat. I know beige from wheat." And I said, "Well, my dear, I know beige from wheat, too." What did I say? What did I just say?

DADDY. (*Tonelessly.*) Well, my dear, I know beige from wheat, too.

MOMMY. That's right. And she laughed, and she said, "Well, my dear, they certainly put one over on you; that's wheat if I ever saw wheat. But it's lovely, just the same." And then she walked off. She's a dreadful woman, you don't know her; she has dreadful taste, two dreadful children, a dreadful house, and an absolutely adorable husband who sits in a wheelchair all the time. You don't know him. You don't know anybody, do you? She's just a dreadful woman, but she *is* chairman of our woman's club, so naturally, I'm terribly fond of her. So, I went right back into the hat shop, and I said, "Look here; what do you mean selling me a hat that you say is beige, when it's wheat all the time; wheat. I can tell beige from wheat any day in the week, but not in this artificial light of yours." They have artificial light, Daddy.

DADDY. Have they!

MOMMY. And I said, "The minute I got outside I could tell that it wasn't a beige hat at all; it was a wheat hat." And they said to me, "How could you tell that when you had the hat on the top of your head?" Well, that made me angry, and so I made a scene right there; (*Rises and crosses to Daddy.*) I screamed as hard as I could; I took my hat off, and I threw it down on the counter, and oh I made a terrible scene. I said, I made a terrible scene.

DADDY. (*Snapping to.*) Yes . . . yes . . . good for you.

MOMMY. And I made an absolutely terrible scene; and they became frightened, and they said, "Oh, Madam, oh, Madam." But I kept right on, and finally they admitted that they might have made a mistake; so they took my hat into the back, and then they came out again with a hat that looked exactly like it. I took one look at it, and I said, "This hat is wheat-colored; wheat." Well, of course, they said, "Oh, no, Madam, this hat is beige; you go outside and see." So, I went outside, and lo and behold, it *was* beige. And so I bought it. (*Crosses to arch R.*)

DADDY. (*Clearing his throat.*) I would imagine that it was the same hat they tried to sell you before.

MOMMY. (*With a little laugh.*) Well, of course it was!

DADDY. That's the way things are today; you just can't get satisfaction; you just try.

MOMMY. Well, *I* got satisfaction.

DADDY. That's right, Mommy. *You did* get satisfaction, didn't you.

MOMMY. Why are they so late? I don't know what can be keeping them.

DADDY. I've been trying for two weeks to have the leak in the johnny fixed.

MOMMY. *You* can't get satisfaction; just try. (*Sits chair R.*) *I* can get satisfaction, but you can't.

DADDY. I've been trying for two weeks and it isn't so much for my sake; I can always go to the club.

MOMMY. It isn't so much for my sake, either; I can always go shopping.

DADDY. It's really for Grandma's sake.

MOMMY. Of course it's for Grandma's sake. Grandma cries every time she goes to the johnny as it is; but now that it doesn't work it's even worse, it makes Grandma think she's getting feeble-headed.

DADDY. Grandma *is* getting feeble-headed.

MOMMY. Of course Grandma is getting feeble-headed, but not about her johnny-dos.

DADDY. No, that's true. I must have it fixed.

MOMMY. (*Crossing to arch* R.) Why are they so late? I don't know what can be keeping them.

DADDY. When they came here the first time, they were ten minutes early; they were quick enough about it then. (*Enter Grandma from the archway, L. She is loaded down with boxes, large and small, neatly wrapped and tied.*)

MOMMY. Why, Grandma; look at you! What *is* all that you're carrying?

GRANDMA. They're boxes. What do they look like?

MOMMY. Daddy! Look at Grandma; look at all the boxes she's carrying!

DADDY. My goodness, Grandma; look at all those boxes.

GRANDMA. Where'll I put them?

MOMMY. Heavens! I don't know. Whatever are they for?

GRANDMA. That's nobody's damn business.

MOMMY. Well, in that case, put them down next to Daddy, there.

GRANDMA. (*Dumping the boxes down, on and around Daddy's feet.*) I sure wish you'd get the john fixed. (*Exit archway, L.*)

DADDY. Oh, I do wish they'd come and fix it. We hear you . . . for hours . . . whimpering away. . . .

MOMMY. Daddy! What a terrible thing to say to Grandma!

GRANDMA. (*Re-entering with more boxes.*) Yeah. For shame, talking to me that way.

DADDY. I'm sorry.

MOMMY. Daddy's sorry, Grandma. (*Sits chair* R.)

GRANDMA. Well, all right. In that case I'll go get the rest of the boxes. I suppose I deserve being talked to that way, I've gotten so old. Most people think that when you get so old, you

10

either freeze to death, or you burn up. But you don't. When you get so old, all that happens is that people talk to you that way.

DADDY. (*Contrite.*) I said I'm sorry, Grandma.

MOMMY. Daddy said he was sorry.

GRANDMA. Well, that's all that counts. People being sorry. Makes you feel better; gives you a sense of dignity, and that's all that's important; a sense of dignity. And it doesn't matter if you don't care, or not, either. You got to have a sense of dignity, even if you don't care, 'cause, if you don't have that, civilization's doomed.

MOMMY. (*Crossing to Grandma.*) You've been reading my book club selections again!

DADDY. How dare you read Mommy's book club selections, Grandma!

GRANDMA. Because I'm old! When you're old you gotta do something. When you get old, you can't talk to people because people snap at you. When you get so old, people talk to you that way. (*Mommy sits chair,* R. *Grandma crosses to her.*) That's why you become deaf, so you won't be able to hear people talking to you that way. And that's why you go and hide under the covers in the big soft bed, so you won't feel the house shaking from people talking to you that way. (*Crossing to Daddy.*) That's why old people die, eventually. People talk to them that way. I've got to go and get the rest of the boxes. (*Grandma exits,* L.)

DADDY. Poor Grandma, I didn't mean to hurt her.

MOMMY. Don't you worry about it; Grandma doesn't know what she means.

DADDY. She knows what she says, though.

MOMMY. Don't you worry about it; she won't know that soon. I love Grandma.

DADDY. I love her too. Look how nicely she wrapped these boxes.

MOMMY. Grandma has always wrapped boxes nicely. When I was a little girl, I was very poor, and Grandma was very poor, too, because Grandpa was in heaven. And every day, when I went to school Grandma used to wrap a box for me, and I used to take it with me to school; and when it was lunch time, all the little boys and girls used to take out their boxes of lunch, and they weren't wrapped nicely at all, and they used to open them and eat their chicken legs and chocolate cakes; and I used

11

to say, "Oh, look at my lovely lunch box; it's so nicely wrapped it would break my heart to open it." And so, I wouldn't open it.

DADDY. Because it was empty.

MOMMY. Oh, no. Grandma always filled it up, because she never ate the dinner she cooked the evening before; she gave me all her food for my lunch box the next day. After school, I'd take the box back to Grandma, and she'd open it and eat the chicken legs and chocolate cake that was inside. Grandma used to say, "I love day-old cake." That's where the expression 'day-old cake' came from. Grandma always ate everything a day late. I used to eat all the other little boys' and girls' food at school, because they thought my lunch box was empty. They thought my lunch box was empty, and that's why I wouldn't open it. They thought I suffered from the sin of pride, and since that made them better than me, they were very generous.

DADDY. You were a very deceitful little girl.

MOMMY. We were very poor! But then I married you, Daddy, and now we're very rich.

DADDY. Grandma isn't rich.

MOMMY. (Rising, to C.) No, but you've been so good to Grandma she feels rich. She doesn't know you'd like to put her in a nursing home.

DADDY. I wouldn't!

MOMMY. Well, heaven knows, I would! I can't stand it, watching her do the cooking and the housework, polishing the silver, moving the furniture. . . .

DADDY. She likes to do that. She says it's the least she can do to earn her keep.

MOMMY. Well, she's right. You can't live off people. I can live off you, because I married you. And aren't you lucky all I brought with me was Grandma. A lot of women I know would have brought their whole families to live off you. All I brought was Grandma. Grandma is all the family I have.

DADDY. I feel very fortunate.

MOMMY. You should. I have a right to live off of you because I married you, and because I used to let you get on top of me and bump your uglies; and I have a right to all your money when you die. And when you do, Grandma and I can live by ourselves . . . if she's still here. Unless you have her put away in a nursing home.

12

DADDY. I have no intention of putting her in a nursing home.

MOMMY. (*Crossing to arch* R.) Well, I wish somebody would do something with her.

DADDY. At any rate, you're very well provided for.

MOMMY. (*Crosses to Daddy.*) You're my sweet Daddy; that's very nice.

DADDY. I love my Mommy. (*Enter Grandma again* L., *laden with more boxes.*)

GRANDMA. (*Dumping the boxes on and around Daddy's feet.*) There; that's the lot of them.

DADDY. They're wrapped so nicely.

GRANDMA. (*To Daddy.*) You won't get on my sweet side that way.

MOMMY. Grandma!

GRANDMA. . . . telling me how nicely I wrap boxes. Not after what you said: how I whimpered for hours. . . .

MOMMY. Grandma!

GRANDMA. (*To Mommy.*) Shut up. (*Mommy crosses to arch* R. *To Daddy.*) You don't have any feelings, that's what's wrong with you. Old people make all sorts of noises, half of them they can't help. Old people whimper, and cry, and belch, and make great hollow rumbing sounds at table; old people wake up in the middle of the night screaming, and find out they haven't even been asleep; and when old people *are* asleep, they try to wake up, and they can't . . . not for the longest time.

MOMMY. Homilies; homilies! (*Sits chair* R.)

GRANDMA. (*To Mommy.*) And there's more, too.

DADDY. I'm really very sorry, Grandma.

GRANDMA. I know you are Daddy; it's Mommy over there makes all the trouble. (*Sits on big box* R. *of Daddy.*) If you'd listened to me you wouldn't have married her in the first place. She was a tramp and a trollop and a trull to boot, and she's no better now.

MOMMY. (*Rises.*) Grandma!

GRANDMA. (*To Mommy.*) Shut up. (*Mommy sits. To Daddy.*) When she was no more than eight years old she used to climb up on my lap and say, in a sickening little voice, "When I gwo up, I'm going to mahwy a wich old man; I'm going to set my wittle were end right down in a tub o' butter; that's what I'm going to do." And I warned you Daddy; I told you to stay away

13

from her type. I told you to. I did. (*Mommy crosses to Grandma, pulling her up and pushing her* D. R.)

MOMMY. You stop that! You're *my* mother, not his!

GRANDMA. I am?

DADDY. That's right, Grandma, Mommy's right.

GRANDMA. Well, how would you expect somebody as old as I am to remember a thing like that? You don't make allowances for people. (*Crossing* L. *to Daddy.*) I want an allowance. I want an allowance!

DADDY. All right, Grandma; I'll see to it.

MOMMY. Grandma! I'm ashamed of you.

GRANDMA. (*Running from Mommy around to* R. *of sofa.*) Humf!! It's a fine time to say that. You should have gotten rid of me a long time ago if that's the way you feel. You should have had Daddy set me up in business somewhere . . . I could have gone into the fur business, or I could have been a singer. (*Mommy crossing after Grandma around sofa.*) But no; not you. You wanted me around so you could sleep in my room when Daddy got fresh. But now it isn't important, because Daddy doesn't want to get fresh with you anymore, and I don't blame him. (*Grandma crosses* D. L. *of Daddy.*) You'd rather sleep with me, wouldn't you Daddy?

MOMMY. (*Mommy,* R. *of Daddy.*) Daddy doesn't want to sleep with anyone. Daddy's been sick.

DADDY. I've been sick. I don't even want to sleep in the apartment.

MOMMY. You see? I told you.

DADDY. I just want to get everything over with.

MOMMY. That's right. (*Crossing to arch* R.) Why are they so late? Why can't they get here on time?

GRANDMA. (*Crossing to Mommy. An owl.*) Who? Who? . . . Who? Who?

MOMMY. You know, Grandma.

GRANDMA. No, I don't.

MOMMY. (*Sits chair* R.) Well, it doesn't really matter whether you do, or not.

DADDY. Is that true?

MOMMY. Oh, more or less. Look how pretty Grandma wrapped these boxes.

14

GRANDMA. (*Sits on sofa.*) I didn't really like wrapping them; it hurt my fingers, and it frightened me. But, it had to be done.

MOMMY. Why, Grandma?

GRANDMA. None of your damn business.

MOMMY. Go to bed.

GRANDMA. I don't want to go to bed. I just got up. I want to stay here and watch. Besides. . . .

MOMMY. Go to bed.

DADDY. Let her stay up, Mommy; it isn't noon yet.

GRANDMA. (*Crosses to Daddy.*) I want to watch; besides. . . .

DADDY. Let her watch, Mommy.

MOMMY. Well, all right, you can watch; but don't you dare say a word.

GRANDMA. Old people are very good at listening; old people don't like to talk; (*Mommy starts for Grandma who crosses* D. L.) old people have colitis and lavender perfume. Now I'm going to be quiet.

DADDY. She never mentioned she wanted to be a singer.

MOMMY. Oh, I forgot to tell you, but it was ages ago. (*The doorbell rings.*) Oh, goodness! Here they are!

GRANDMA. (*Crossing to Mommy,* C.) Who? Who?

MOMMY. Oh, just some people.

GRANDMA. The van people? Is it the van people? Have you finally done it? Have you called the van people to come and take me away?

DADDY. Of course not, Grandma!

GRANDMA. Oh, don't be too sure. She'd have you carted off, too, if she thought she could get away with it.

MOMMY. Pay no attention to her, Daddy. (*An aside to Grandma.*) My God, you're ungrateful! (*The doorbell rings again.*)

DADDY. (*Wringing his hands.*) Oh, dear; oh, dear.

MOMMY. (*Still to Grandma.*) Just you wait; I'll fix your wagon. (*Now, to Daddy.*) Well, go let them in, Daddy. What are you waiting for?

DADDY. I think we should talk about it some more. Maybe we've been hasty . . . a little hasty, perhaps. (*Doorbell rings again.*) I'd like to talk about it some more.

MOMMY. There's no need. You made up your mind; you were firm; you were masculine and decisive.

15

DADDY. We might consider the pros and the . . .

MOMMY. I won't argue with you; it has to be done; you were right. Open the door.

DADDY. But I'm not sure that. . . .

MOMMY. (*Pushing Daddy up out of his chair.*) Open the door.

DADDY. (*Crosses to arch* R., *thinks better of it, turns back to Mommy.*) Was I firm about it?

MOMMY. Oh, so firm; so firm.

DADDY. And was I decisive?

MOMMY. So decisive! Oh, I shivered.

DADDY. And masculine? Was I really masculine?

MOMMY. Oh, Daddy, you were so masculine; I shivered and fainted.

GRANDMA. (*Sits chair* L.) Shivered and fainted, did she? Humf!

MOMMY. You be quiet.

GRANDMA. Old people have a right to talk to themselves; it doesn't hurt the gums, and it's comforting. (*Doorbell rings again.*)

DADDY. (*Crosses to arch* R.) I shall now open the door.

MOMMY. What a masculine Daddy! (*To Grandma.*) Isn't he a masculine Daddy?

GRANDMA. Don't expect me to say anything. Old people are obscene.

MOMMY. Some of your opinions aren't so bad. You know that?

DADDY. (*Backing off from the door.*) Maybe we can send them away.

MOMMY. Oh, look at you! You're turning into jelly; you're indecisive; you're a woman.

DADDY. All right. Watch me now; I'm going to open the door. Watch. Watch!

MOMMY. We're watching; we're watching.

GRANDMA. (*Rises, stands* D. L.) *I'm* not.

DADDY. Watch now; it's opening! (*He opens the door.*) It's open! (*Mrs. Barker steps into the room.*) Here they are!

MOMMY. Here they are!

GRANDMA. Where?

DADDY. Come in. You're late. But, of course, we expected you to be late; we were saying that we expected you to be late.

MOMMY. (*Crossing to Mrs. Barker.*) Daddy, don't be rude! We were saying that you just can't get satisfaction these days, and we were talking about you, of course. Won't you come in?

MRS. BARKER. (*Crosses* C.) Thank you; I don't mind if I do.

MOMMY. We're very glad that you're here, late as you are. You do remember us, don't you? You were here once before. I'm Mommy, and this is Daddy, and that's Grandma, doddering there in the corner.

MRS. BARKER. Hello, Mommy; hello, Daddy; and hello there, Grandma.

DADDY. Now that you're here, I don't suppose you could go away and maybe come back some other time.

MRS. BARKER. Oh, no; we're much too efficient for that. I said, hello there, Grandma.

MOMMY. Speak to them, Grandma.

GRANDMA. I don't see them.

DADDY. For shame, Grandma; they're here.

MRS. BARKER. Yes, we're here, Grandma. I'm Mrs. Barker. I remember you; don't you remember me?

GRANDMA. I don't recall; maybe you were younger, or something.

MOMMY. Grandma! What a terrible thing to say!

MRS. BARKER. Oh, now, don't scold her, Mommy; for all she knows she may be right.

DADDY. Uh . . . Mrs. Barker, is it? Won't you sit down?

MRS. BARKER. (*Sits sofa.*) I don't mind if I do.

MOMMY. Would you like a cigarette, and a drink, and would you like to cross your legs?

MRS. BARKER. You forget yourself, Mommy; I'm a professional woman. But I will cross my legs.

DADDY. (*Sits chair* L. *Mommy sits chair* R.) Yes, make yourself comfortable.

MRS. BARKER. I don't mind if I do. (*Pause.*)

GRANDMA. Are they still here?

MOMMY. Be quiet, Grandma.

MRS. BARKER. Oh, we're still here. My, what an unattractive apartment you have.

MOMMY. Yes, but you don't know what a trouble it is. Let me tell you. . . .

DADDY. I was saying to Mommy. . . .

MRS. BARKER. Yes, I know. I was listening outside.

DADDY. About the icebox, and . . . the doorbell . . . and the . . .

17

MRS. BARKER. . . . and the johnny. Yes, we're very efficient; we have to know everything in our work.

DADDY. Exactly what do you do?

MOMMY. Yes, what is your work?

MRS. BARKER. Well, my dear, for one thing I'm chairman of your women's club.

MOMMY. (*Crosses to Mrs. Barker.*) Don't be ridiculous. I was talking to the chairman of my women's club just yester . . . why, so you are. (*Crosses to Daddy.*) You remember, Daddy, the lady I was telling you about? The lady with the husband who sits in the *swing*? Don't you remember?

DADDY. No. . . . no . . .

MOMMY. Of course you do. I'm so sorry, Mrs. Barker. I would have known you anywhere, except in this artificial light. (*Crossing around sofa to* R.) And look! You have a hat just like the one I bought yesterday.

MRS. BARKER. (*With a little laugh.*) No, not really; this hat is cream.

MOMMY. Well, my dear, that may look like a cream hat to you, but I can . . .

MRS. BARKER. Now, now; you seem to forget who I am.

MOMMY. Yes, I do, don't I? Are you sure you're comfortable? Won't you take off your dress?

MRS. BARKER. I don't mind if I do. (*Mrs. Barker removes her dress. Mommy lays it neatly over sofa back.*)

MOMMY. (*Mommy sits chair* R. *Mrs. Barker sits sofa.*) There; you must feel a great deal more comfortable.

MRS. BARKER. Well, I certainly *look* a great deal more comfortable.

DADDY. I'm going to blush and giggle.

MOMMY. Daddy's going to blush and giggle.

MRS. BARKER. (*Pulling the hem of her slip above her knees. Daddy giggles.*) You're lucky to have such a man for a husband.

MOMMY. Oh, don't I know it!

DADDY. I just blushed and giggled.

MOMMY. Isn't Daddy a caution, Mrs. Barker?

MRS. BARKER. Maybe if I smoked . . . ?

MOMMY. Oh, that isn't necessary.

MRS. BARKER. I don't mind if I do.

MOMMY. No; no, don't, really.

MRS. BARKER. I don't mind. . . .

MOMMY. (*Rising and crossing to Mrs. Barker.*) I won't have you smoking in my house, and that's that! You're a professional woman.

DADDY. Grandma drinks AND smokes; don't you, Grandma?

GRANDMA. No.

MOMMY. (*Crosses L. into boxes.*) Well, now, Mrs. Barker; suppose you tell us why you're here.

GRANDMA. (*As Mommy walks through the boxes.*) The boxes . . . the boxes.

MOMMY. Be quiet, Grandma.

DADDY. What did you say, Grandma?

GRANDMA. (*As Mommy steps on several of the boxes.*) The boxes, damn it!

MRS. BARKER. Boxes; she said boxes. She mentioned the boxes.

DADDY. What about the boxes, Grandma? Maybe Mrs. Barker is here because of the boxes. Is that what you meant, Grandma?

GRANDMA. I don't know if that's what I meant, or not. It's certainly not what I *thought* I meant.

DADDY. Grandma is of the opinion that . . .

MRS. BARKER. Can we assume that the boxes are for us? I mean, can we assume that you had us come here for the boxes?

MOMMY. Are you in the habit of receiving boxes?

DADDY. A very good question.

MRS. BARKER. Well, that would depend on the reason we're here. I've got my fingers in so many little pies, you know. Now, I can think of one of my little activities in which we are in the habit of receiving *baskets*, but more in a literary sense than really. We *might* receive boxes, though, under very special circumstances. I'm afraid that's the best answer I can give you.

DADDY. It's a very interesting answer.

MRS. BARKER. *I* thought so. But, does it help?

MOMMY. (*Sits chair R.*) No; I'm afraid not.

DADDY. I wonder if it might help us any if I said I feel misgivings, that I have definite qualms.

MOMMY. Where, Daddy?

DADDY. (*Unbuttoning his jacket and indicating stitches.*) Well, mostly right here, right around where the stitches were.

MOMMY. Daddy had an operation, you know.

MRS. BARKER. Oh, you poor Daddy! I didn't know; but, then how could I?

19

GRANDMA. (*Crossing to Mrs. Barker.*) You might have asked; it wouldn't have hurt you.

MOMMY. Dry up, Grandma.

GRANDMA. There you go. Letting your true feelings come out. Old people aren't dry enough, I suppose. My sacks are empty, the fluid in my eyeballs is all caked on the inside edges, my spine is made of sugar candy, I breathe ice; but you don't hear me complain. Nobody hears old people complain because people think that's all old people do. And *that's* because old people are gnarled and sagged and twisted into the shape of a complaint. (*Signs off.*) That's all. (*Crosses D. L.*)

MRS. BARKER. What was wrong, Daddy?

DADDY. Well, you know how it is: the doctors took out something that was there and put in something that wasn't there. An operation.

MRS. BARKER. You're very fortunate, I should say.

MOMMY. Oh, he is; he is. All his life, Daddy has wanted to be a United States Senator; but now . . . why, now he's changed his mind, and for the rest of his life he's going to want to be governor . . . it would be nearer the apartment, you know.

MRS. BARKER. You *are* fortunate, Daddy.

DADDY. Yes, indeed; except that I get these qualms now and then, definite ones.

MRS. BARKER. Well, it's just a matter of things settling; you're like an old house.

MOMMY. Why Daddy, thank Mrs. Barker.

DADDY. Thank you.

MRS. BARKER. Ambition! That's the ticket. I have a brother who's very much like you, Daddy . . . ambitious. Of course, he's a great deal younger than you; he's even younger than I am . . . if such a thing is possible. He runs a little newspaper. Just a little newspaper . . . but he runs it. He's chief cook and bottle washer of that little newspaper, which he calls The Village Idiot. He has such a sense of humor; he's so self-deprecating, so modest. And he'd never admit it himself, but he *is* The Village Idiot.

MOMMY. Oh, I think that's just grand. Don't you think so, Daddy?

DADDY. Yes, just grand.

MRS. BARKER. My brother's a dear man, and he has a dear

20

little wife, whom he loves, dearly. He loves her so much he just can't get a sentence out without mentioning her. He wants everybody to know he's married. He's really a stickler on that point; he can't be introduced to anybody and say "hello" without adding "of course, I'm married." As far as I'm concerned, he's the chief exponent of Woman Love in this whole country; he's even been written up in psychiatric journals because of it.

DADDY. Indeed!

MOMMY. Isn't that lovely.

MRS. BARKER. Oh I think so. There's too much woman-hatred in this country, and that's a fact.

GRANDMA. Oh, I don't know.

MOMMY. Oh, I think that's just grand. Don't you think so, Daddy?

DADDY. Yes, just grand.

GRANDMA. (*Crossing* L. C.) In case anybody's interested. . . .

MOMMY. Be quiet, Grandma.

GRANDMA. Nuts! (*Turns her back on the group.*)

MOMMY. Oh, Mrs. Barker, you *must* forgive Grandma. She's rural.

MRS. BARKER. I don't mind if I do.

DADDY. Maybe Grandma has something to say.

MOMMY. Nonsense. Old people have nothing to say; and if old people *did* have something to say, nobody would listen to them. (*Rises. To Grandma.*) You see? I can pull that stuff just as easy as you can.

GRANDMA. Well, you got the rhythm, but you don't really have the quality. Besides, you're middle-aged.

MOMMY. I'm proud of it.

GRANDMA. Look. I'll show you how it's really done. Middle-aged people think they can do anything, but the truth is that middle-aged people can't do most things as well as they used to. Middle-aged people think they're special because they're like everybody else. We live in the age of deformity. You see? Rhythm *and* content. You'll learn. (*Crosses* D. L.)

DADDY. I do wish I weren't surrounded by women, I'd like some men around here.

MRS. BARKER. You can say that again!

GRANDMA. I don't hardly count as a woman, so can I say my piece?

21

MOMMY. (*Sits chair* R.) Go on. Jabber away.

GRANDMA. It's very simple; the fact is, these boxes don't have anything to do with why this good lady is come to call. Now if you're interested in knowing why these boxes *are* here. . . .

DADDY. I'm sure that must be all very true, Grandma, but what does it have to do with why . . . pardon me, what is that name again?

MRS. BARKER. Mrs. Barker.

DADDY. Exactly. What does it have to do with why . . . that name again?

MRS. BARKER. Mrs. Barker.

DADDY. Precisely. What does it have to do with why what's-her-name is here?

MOMMY. They're here because we asked them.

MRS. BARKER. Yes. That's why.

GRANDMA. Now, if you're interested in knowing why these boxes *are* here. . . .

MOMMY. Well, nobody *is* interested!

GRANDMA. (*Crossing* R. *To Mommy.*) You can be as snippity as you like for all the good it'll do you.

DADDY. You two will have to stop arguing.

MOMMY. (*Crossing to Daddy.*) I don't argue with her.

DADDY. It will just have to stop.

MOMMY. Well, why don't you call a van and have her taken away?

GRANDMA. Don't bother; there's no need.

DADDY. No, now, perhaps I can go away myself. . . .

MOMMY. Well, one or the other; the way things are now it's impossible. In the first place, it's too crowded in this apartment. (*To Grandma.*) And it's you that takes up all the space, with your enema bottles, and your Pekinese, and God-only-knows what else . . . and now all these boxes. . . . (*Kicking the boxes.*)

GRANDMA. These boxes are . . .

MRS. BARKER. I've never heard of enema *bottles*. . . .

GRANDMA. She means enema bags, but she doesn't know the difference. Mommy comes from extremely bad stock. And, besides, when Mommy was born . . . well, it was a difficult delivery, and she had a head shaped like a banana.

MOMMY. You ungrateful . . . Daddy? Daddy, you see how ungrateful she is after all these years, after all the things we've done for her? (*To Grandma.*) One of these days you're going away in a van; that's what's going to happen to you!

GRANDMA. Do tell!

MRS. BARKER. Like a banana?

GRANDMA. Yup, just like a banana.

MRS. BARKER. My word!

MOMMY. You stop listening to her; she'll say anything. Just the other night she called Daddy a hedgehog.

MRS. BARKER. She didn't!

GRANDMA. That's right, baby; you stick up for me.

MOMMY. I don't know where she gets the words; on the television, maybe.

MRS. BARKER. Did you really call him a hedgehog?

GRANDMA. (*Crossing D. R.*) Oh, look; what difference does it make whether I did or not?

DADDY. Grandma's right. Leave Grandma alone.

MOMMY. (*To Daddy.*) How dare you!

GRANDMA. Oh, leave her alone, Daddy; the kid's all mixed up.

MOMMY. You see? I told you. It's all those television shows. Daddy, you go right into Grandma's room and take her television and shake all the tubes loose.

DADDY. Don't mention tubes to me.

MOMMY. Oh! Mommy forgot! (*To Mrs. Barker.*) Daddy has tubes now where he used to have tracts.

MRS. BARKER. Is that a fact!

GRANDMA. (*Crossing to Mrs. Barker.*) I know why this dear lady is here.

MOMMY. You be still.

MRS. BARKER. (*Rising. To Grandma.*) Oh, I do wish you'd tell me.

MOMMY. No! No! That wouldn't be fair at all.

DADDY. Besides, she knows why she's here; she's here because we called them.

MRS. BARKER. (*Crossing L. to Daddy.*) La! But that still leaves me puzzled. I know I'm here because you called us, but I'm such a busy girl, with this committee and that committee, and the Responsible Citizens Activities I indulge in.

MOMMY. Oh my; busy, busy.

MRS. BARKER. Yes, indeed. So, I'm afraid you'll have to give me some help.

23

MOMMY. Oh, no. No, you must be mistaken. I can't believe we asked you here to give you any help. With the way taxes are these days, and the way you can't get satisfaction in ANYTHING. . . . No, I don't believe so.

DADDY. And if you need help . . . why, I should think you'd apply for a Fulbright Scholarship. . . .

MOMMY. And if not that . . . why, then a Guggenheim Fellowship. . . .

GRANDMA. Oh, come on; why not shoot the works and try the Ford Foundation. (*Under her breath, to Mommy and Daddy.*) Beasts! (*Crosses* D. R.)

MRS. BARKER. Oh, what a jolly family. (*Crosses* R.) But let me think. I'm knee-deep in work these days; there's the Ladies Auxiliary Air-Raid Committee, for one thing; (*To Daddy.*) how do you feel about air-raids?

MOMMY. Oh, I'd say we're hostile.

DADDY. Yes, definitely; we're hostile.

MRS. BARKER. Then you'll be no help there. There's too much hostility in the world these days, as it is; but I'll not badger you. There's a surfeit of badgers, as well. (*Sits chair* R.)

GRANDMA. While we're at it, there's been a run on old people, too. The Department of Agriculture, or maybe it wasn't the Department of Agriculture . . . anyway, it was some department that's run by a girl, put out figures showing that ninety per cent of the adult population of the country is over eighty years old . . . or eighty per cent is over ninety years old. . . .

MOMMY. You're such a liar! You just finished saying that everyone is middle-aged.

GRANDMA. (*Crosses* C. *to Mommy.*) I'm just telling you what the government says . . . that doesn't have anything to do with what . . .

MOMMY. It's that television! Daddy, go break her television.

GRANDMA. You won't find it.

DADDY. (*Wearily getting up.*) If I must. . . . I must.

MOMMY. And don't step on the Pekinese; it's blind.

DADDY. It may be blind, but Daddy isn't. (*He exits, through the archway,* L.)

GRANDMA. (*Crossing to* L. *arch after Daddy.*) You won't find it, either.

MOMMY. (*Crosses to Mrs. Barker,* R.) Oh, I'm so fortunate to

24

have such a husband. Just think: I could have had a husband who was poor, or argumentative, or a husband who sat in a wheelchair all day. (*Mrs. Barker rises.*) . . . OOOOHHHH! *What* have I said? What *have* I said?

GRANDMA. You said you could have a husband who sat in a wheel . . .

MOMMY. (*Starting after Grandma who sits chair, L.*) I'm mortified! I could die! I could cut my tongue out! I could . . .

MRS. BARKER. (*Forcing a smile.*) Oh, now . . . now . . . don't think about it. . . .

MOMMY. (*Crosses to Mrs. Barker.*) I could . . . why, I could . . .

MRS. BARKER. . . . don't think about it . . . really . . .

MOMMY. You're quite right. I won't think about it, and that way I'll forget that I ever said it, and that way it will be all right. (*Pause.*) There . . . I've forgotten. (*Pulling Mrs. Barker to sofa, both sit.*) Well, now, now that Daddy is out of the room we can have some girl talk.

MRS. BARKER. I'm not sure that I . . .

MOMMY. You *do* want to have some girl talk, don't you?

MRS. BARKER. I was going to say I'm not sure that I wouldn't care for a glass of water. I feel a little faint.

MOMMY. Grandma, go get Mrs. Barker a glass of water.

GRANDMA. —I would prefer not to.

MOMMY. Grandma loves to do little things around the house; it gives her a false sense of security.

GRANDMA. I quit! I'm through! (*Begins to stack boxes.*)

MOMMY. Now, you be a good Grandma, or you know what will happen to you. You'll be taken away in a van.

GRANDMA. (*Crossing up to Mommy.*) You don't frighten me. I'm too old to be frightened. And besides . . .

MOMMY. WELL! I'll tend to you later. I'll hide your teeth . . . I'll . . .

GRANDMA. Everything's hidden.

MRS. BARKER. I *am* going to faint. I *am*.

MOMMY. (*Rises.*) Good heavens! I'll go myself. (*As she exits, through the archway, L.*) I'll fix you Grandma. I'll take care of you later. (*She exits.*)

GRANDMA. Oh, go soak your head. (*To Mrs. Barker.*) Well, dearie, how do you feel? (*Sits next to Mrs. Barker on Sofa.*)

25

MRS. BARKER. A little better, I think. Yes, much better, thank you, Grandma.

GRANDMA. That's good.

MRS. BARKER. But . . . I feel so lost . . . not knowing why I'm here . . . and, on top of it, they say I was here before.

GRANDMA. Well, you were. You weren't *here,* exactly, because we've moved around a lot, from one apartment to another, up and down the social ladder like mice, if you like similes.

MRS. BARKER. I don't . . . particularly.

GRANDMA. (*Rises. Resumes stacking boxes.*) Well, then, I'm sorry.

MRS. BARKER. (*Rises. Suddenly.*) Grandma, I feel I can trust you.

GRANDMA. Don't be too sure; it's every man for himself around this place. . . .

MRS. BARKER. Oh . . . is it? Nonetheless, I really do feel that I can trust you. *Please* tell me why they called and asked us to come. I implore you!

GRANDMA. Oh my; that feels good. It's been so long since anybody implored me. Do it again. Implore me some more.

MRS. BARKER. (*Crosses* R.) You're your daughter's mother all right!

GRANDMA. (*Crossing to Mrs. Barker.*) Oh, I don't mean to be hard. If you won't implore me, then beg me, or ask me, or entreat me . . . just anything like that.

MRS. BARKER. You're a dreadful old woman!

GRANDMA. (*Resumes stacking boxes.*) You'll understand some day. Please!

MRS. BARKER. Oh, for heavens sake! . . . I implore you . . . I beg you . . . I beseech you! (*Sits chair* R.)

GRANDMA. (*Crosses* R., *to Mrs. Barker.*) Beseech! Oh, that's the nicest word I've heard in ages. You're a dear, sweet woman . . . You . . . beseech . . . me. I can't resist that.

MRS. BARKER. Well then . . . please tell me why they asked us to come.

GRANDMA. (*Checks through arch* L., *then crosses to Mrs. Barker.*) Well, I'll give you a hint. That's the best I can do, because I'm a muddle-headed old woman. Now listen, because it's important. Once upon a time, not too very long ago, but a long enough time ago . . . oh, about twenty years ago. . . . there was a

26

man very much like Daddy, and a woman very much like Mommy, who were married to each other, very much like Mommy and Daddy are married to each other; and they lived in an apartment very much like one that's very much like this one, and they lived there with an old woman who was very much like yours truly, only younger, because it was some time ago; in fact, they were all somewhat younger.

MRS. BARKER. How fascinating!

GRANDMA. Now, at the same time, there was a dear lady very much like you, only younger then, who did all sorts of Good Works. . . . And one of the Good Works this dear lady did was in something very much like a volunteer capacity for an organization very much like the Bye-Bye Adoption Service, which is nearby and which was run by a terribly deaf old lady very much like the Miss Bye-Bye who runs the Bye-Bye Adoption Service nearby.

MRS. BARKER. How enthralling!

GRANDMA. (*Crossing* L., *then back to Mrs. Barker.*) Well, be that as it may. Nonetheless, one afternoon this man, who was very much like Daddy, and this woman who was very much like Mommy came to see this dear lady who did all the Good Works, who was very much like you, dear, and they were very sad and very hopeful, and they cried and smiled and bit their fingers, and they said all the most intimate things.

MRS. BARKER. How spellbinding! What did they say?

GRANDMA. Well, it was very sweet. The woman, who was very much like Mommy, said that she and the man, who was very much like Daddy, had never been blessed with anything very much like a bumble of joy.

MRS. BARKER. A what?

GRANDMA. A bumble; a bumble of joy.

MRS. BARKER. Oh, like a bundle.

GRANDMA. Well, yes; very much like it. Bundle, bumble; who cares? At any rate, the woman, who was very much like Mommy, said that they wanted a bumble of their own, but that the man, who was very much like Daddy, couldn't have a bumble; and the man, who was very much like Daddy, said that yes, they had wanted a bumble of their own, but that the woman, who was very much like Mommy, couldn't have one, and that now they wanted to buy something very much like a bumble.

MRS. BARKER. How engrossing!

GRANDMA. Yes. And the dear lady, who was very much like you, said something that was very much like, "Oh, what a shame; but take heart; I think we have just the bumble for you." And, well, the lady, who was very much like Mommy, and the man, who was very much like Daddy, cried and smiled and bit their fingers, and said some more intimate things, which were totally irrelevant, but which were pretty hot stuff, and so the dear lady, who was very much like you, and who had something very much like a penchant for pornography, listened with something very much like enthusiasm. "Whee!" she said. "Whoooopeeeee!" But that's beside the point.

MRS. BARKER. I suppose so. But, how gripping!

GRANDMA. Anyway . . . they *bought* something very much like a bumble, and they took it away with them. But . . . things didn't work out very well.

MRS. BARKER. You mean there was trouble?

GRANDMA. You got it. (*With a glance through the archway.*) But, I'm going to have to speed up now because I think I'm leaving soon.

MRS. BARKER. (*Rises and crosses* c.) Oh. Are you really?

GRANDMA. Yup.

MRS. BARKER. But, old people don't go anywhere; they're either taken places, or put places.

GRANDMA. Well, this old person is different. (*Both sit on sofa.*) Anyway . . . things started going badly.

MRS. BARKER. Oh, yes. Yes.

GRANDMA. Weeeeeellll . . . in the first place, it turned out the bumble didn't look like either one of it's parents. That was enough of a blow, but things got worse. One night, it cried its heart out, if you can imagine such a thing.

MRS. BARKER. Cried its heart out! Well!

GRANDMA. But that was only the beginning. Then it turned out it only had eyes for its Daddy.

MRS. BARKER. For its Daddy! Why, any self-respecting woman would have gouged those eyes right out of its head.

GRANDMA. Well, she did. That's exactly what she did. But then, it kept its nose up in the air.

MRS. BARKER. Ufggh! How disgusting!

28

GRANDMA. That's what they thought. But *then*, it began to develop an interest in its you-know-what.

MRS. BARKER. In its you-know-what! Well! I hope they cut its hands off at the wrists!

GRANDMA. Well, yes, they did that eventually. But first, they cut off its you-know-what.

MRS. BARKER. A much better idea!

GRANDMA. That's what they thought. But after they cut off its you-know-what, it *still* put its hands under the covers, *looking* for its you-know-what. So, finally, they *had* to cut off its hands at the wrists.

MRS. BARKER. Naturally!

GRANDMA. And it was such a resentful bumble. Why, one day it called its Mommy a dirty name.

MRS. BARKER. Well, I hope they cut its tongue out!

GRANDMA. Of course. And, then, as it got bigger, they found out all sorts of terrible things about it, like: it didn't have a head on its shoulders, it had no guts, it was spineless, its feet were made of clay . . . just dreadful things.

MRS. BARKER. Dreadful!

GRANDMA. So you can understand how they became discouraged.

MRS. BARKER. I certainly can! And what did they do?

GRANDMA. What did they do? Well, for the last straw, it finally up and died; and you can imagine how *that* made them feel, their having paid for it and all. So, they called up the lady who sold them the bumble in the first place and told her to come right over to their apartment. They wanted satisfaction; they wanted their money back. That's what they wanted.

MRS. BARKER. My, my, my.

GRANDMA. How do you like them apples?

MRS. BARKER. My, my, my.

DADDY. (*Off-stage.*) Mommy? I can't find Grandma's television, and I can't find the Pekinese, either.

MOMMY. (*Off-stage.*) Isn't that funny? And I can't find the water.

GRANDMA. (*Rises and crosses to arch* L.) Heh, heh, heh. I told them everything was hidden.

MRS. BARKER. Did you hide the water, too?

GRANDMA. (*Puzzled.*) No. No. No, I didn't do *that*.

29

MOMMY. (*Off-stage.*) Oh, I found the water, Daddy. It wasn't where I thought it would be at all.

DADDY. (*Off-stage.*) The truth of the matter is, I can't even find Grandma's room.

GRANDMA. (*Sits sofa.*) Heh, heh, heh.

MRS. BARKER. My! You certainly did hide things, didn't you?

GRANDMA. Sure, kid, sure.

MOMMY. (*Still off-stage.*) Did you ever hear of such a thing, Grandma? Daddy can't find your television, (*Entering L., crosses to Grandma.*) and he can't find the Pekinese, and the truth of the matter is he can't even find your room.

GRANDMA. I told you. I hid everything.

MOMMY. Nonsense, Grandma! Just wait until I get my hands on you. You're a trouble-maker; that's what you are.

GRANDMA. (*Rises. Crosses R. and sits R. chair.*) Well, I'll be out of here pretty soon, baby.

MOMMY. (*Following Grandma R.*) Oh, you don't know how right you are! Daddy's been wanting to send you away for a long time now but I've been restraining him. I'll tell you one thing, though. I'm getting sick and tired of this fighting, and I might just let him have his way. Then you'll see what'll happen. Away you'll go; in a van, too. I'll let Daddy call the van man.

GRANDMA. I'm way ahead of you.

MOMMY. How can you be so old and so smug at the same time? You have no sense of proportion.

GRANDMA. You just answered your own question.

MOMMY. Mrs. Barker, I'd much rather you came into the kitchen for that glass of water, what with Grandma out here, and all.

MRS. BARKER. I don't see what Grandma has to do with it; and besides, I don't think you're very polite.

MOMMY. You seem to forget that you're a guest in this house. . . .

GRANDMA. Apartment!

MOMMY. Apartment! And that you're a professional woman. (*Crosses to L. arch.*) So, if you'll be so good as to come into the kitchen, I'll be more than happy to show you where the water is, and where the glass is, and then you can put two and two to-gether, if you're clever enough. (*She vanishes through L. arch.*)

30

MRS. BARKER. (*After a moment's consideration.*) I suppose she's right.

GRANDMA. (*Rises, crosses up to Mrs. Barker.*) Well, that's how it is when people call you up and ask you over to do something for them.

MRS. BARKER. I suppose you're right, too. (*Rises.*) Well, Grandma, it's been very nice talking to you.

GRANDMA. And I've enjoyed listening. (*Mrs. Barker crosses L. to arch, Grandma stops her.*) Say, don't tell Mommy or Daddy that I gave you that hint, will you?

MRS. BARKER. Oh, dear me, the hint! I'd forgotten about it, if you can imagine such a thing. No, I won't breathe a word of it to them.

GRANDMA. (*Crossing to Mrs. Barker L.*) I don't know if it helped you any . . .

MRS. BARKER. I can't tell yet. I'll have to . . . what *is* the word I want? I'll have to relate it . . . that's it . . . I'll have to relate it to certain things that I *know*, and . . . draw . . . conclusions . . . what I'll really have to do is to see if it applies to anything. I mean, after all, I *do* do volunteer work for an adoption service, but it isn't very much *like* the Bye-Bye Adoption Service . . . it *is* the Bye-Bye Adoption Service . . . and while I can remember Mommy and Daddy coming to see me, oh, about twenty years ago, about buying a bumble, I can't quite remember anyone very much *like* Mommy and Daddy coming to see me about buying a bumble. Don't you see? It really presents quite a problem . . . I'll have to think about it . . . mull it . . . but at any rate, it was truly first-class of you to try to help me. Oh, will you still be here after I've had my drink of water?

GRANDMA. Probably . . . I'm not as spry as I used to be.

MRS. BARKER. Oh. Well, I won't say goodbye then.

GRANDMA. No. Don't. (*Mrs. Barker exits, through the archway. Grandma sits on the sofa.*) People don't say good-bye to old people because they think they'll frighten them. Lordy! If they only knew how awful hello, and my, you're looking chipper sounded, they wouldn't say those things either. (*Rises and starts stacking rest of boxes.*) The truth is, there isn't much you can say to old people that doesn't sound just terrible. (*The doorbell rings.*)

Come on in! (*The Young Man enters,* R. *archway. Grandma looks him over.*) Well, now aren't you a breath of fresh air!

YOUNG MAN. Hello there.

GRANDMA. My, my, my. Are you the van man?

YOUNG MAN. The what?

GRANDMA. (*Crossing to Young Man.*) The van man. The van man. Are you come to take me away?

YOUNG MAN. I don't know what you're talking about. (*Crosses to* L. *arch, looking out.*)

GRANDMA. Oh. (*Pause.*) Well. (*Pause.*) My, my, aren't you something!

YOUNG MAN. Hm?

GRANDMA. I said, my, my; aren't you something.

YOUNG MAN. (*Sits chair* L.) Oh. Thank you.

GRANDMA. You don't sound very enthusiastic.

YOUNG MAN. Oh, I'm . . . I'm used to it.

GRANDMA. (*Sits on arm of chair* L.) Yup; yup; you know, if I were about a hundred and fifty years younger, I could go for you.

YOUNG MAN. Yes, I imagine so.

GRANDMA. Unh-hunh; will you look at those muscles!

YOUNG MAN. (*Rising* C. *and flexing his muscles.*) Yes, they're quite good, aren't they?

GRANDMA. (*Crossing to him.*) Boy, they sure are. They natural?

YOUNG MAN. Well the basic structure was there, but I've done some work too . . . you know, in a gym. (*Sprawls on the sofa.*)

GRANDMA. I'll bet you have. (*Crossing up behind sofa.*) You ought to be in the movies, boy.

YOUNG MAN. I know.

GRANDMA. (*Leaning over back of sofa.*) Yup! Right up there on the old silver screen. But I suppose you've heard that before.

YOUNG MAN. Yes, I have.

GRANDMA. You ought to try out for them . . . the movies.

YOUNG MAN. Well, actually, I may have a career there, yet. I've lived out on the west coast almost all my life . . . and I've met a few people who . . . might be able to help me. (*Sitting up on sofa.*) I'm not in too much of a hurry, though. I'm almost as young as I look.

GRANDMA. (*Crossing* R. *of sofa.*) Oh, that's nice. And will you look at that face!

YOUNG MAN. Yes, it's quite good, isn't it? Clean-cut, midwest farm boy type, almost insultingly good-looking in a typically American way. Good profile, straight nose, honest eyes, wonderful smile. . . .

GRANDMA. Yup. Boy, you know what you are, don't you? You're the American Dream, that's what you are. All those other people they don't know what they're talking about. You . . . *you* are the American Dream.

YOUNG MAN. Thanks.

MOMMY. (*Off-stage.*) Who rang the doorbell?

GRANDMA. (*Shouting off-stage.*) The American Dream!

MOMMY. (*Off-stage.*) What? What was that, Grandma?

GRANDMA. (*Crossing to arch* L. *Shouting.*) The American Dream! The American Dream! Damn it!

DADDY. (*Off-stage.*) How's that, Mommy?

MOMMY. (*Off-stage.*) Oh, some gibberish; pay no attention. Did you find Grandma's room?

DADDY. (*Off-stage.*) I can't find anything.

MOMMY. (*Off-stage.*) All right. I can't find Mrs. Barker.

YOUNG MAN. (*Crossing to Grandma.*) What was all that?

GRANDMA. (*Taking Young Man* C.) Oh, that was just the folks, but let's not talk about them, honey; let's talk about you.

YOUNG MAN. All right.

GRANDMA. (*Sits on sofa.*) Well, let's see. If you're not the van man, what are you doing here?

YOUNG MAN. I'm looking for work.

GRANDMA. Are you! Well; what kind of work?

YOUNG MAN. Oh, almost anything . . . almost anything that pays. I'll do almost anything for money.

GRANDMA. Will you . . . will you. Hmmmm. I wonder if there's anything you could do around here?

YOUNG MAN. There might be. It looked to be a likely building.

GRANDMA. It's always looked to be a rather unlikely building to me, but I suppose you'd know better than I.

YOUNG MAN. (*Crossing behind sofa and leaning over to Grandma.*) I can sense these things.

GRANDMA. There *might* be something you could do around

here. (*As she turns and sees Young Man.*) Stay there! Don't come any closer.

YOUNG MAN. (*Crosses down and sits next to Grandma.*) Sorry.

GRANDMA. I don't mean I'd *mind*. I don't know whether I'd mind, or not. . . . But, it wouldn't look well; it would look just *awful*.

YOUNG MAN. (*Sprawling with his feet in front of Grandma.*) Yes, I suppose so.

GRANDMA. (*Lifting his feet away, Young Man moves to end of sofa.*) Now stay there; let me concentrate. What could you do? The folks have been in something of a quandry around here today, sort of a dilemma, and I wonder if you mightn't be some help.

YOUNG MAN. I hope so . . . if there's money in it. Do you have any money?

GRANDMA. Money! Oh, there's more money around here than you'd know what to do with.

YOUNG MAN. I'm not so sure.

GRANDMA. Well, maybe not. Besides, I've got money of my own.

YOUNG MAN. You have?

GRANDMA. Sure. Old people quite often have lots of money; more often than most people expect. Come here, so I can whisper to you . . . (*As he moves closer.*) not too close. I might faint.

YOUNG MAN. (*Back to his end of sofa.*) Oh, I'm sorry.

GRANDMA. It's all right dear. Anyway . . . have you ever heard of that big baking contest they run? The one where all the ladies get together in a big barn and bake away?

YOUNG MAN. I'm . . . not . . . sure . . .

GRANDMA. Well, it doesn't matter whether you've heard of it or not. The important thing is . . . and I don't want anybody to hear this; the folks think I haven't been out of the house in eight years . . . the important thing is that I won first prize in that baking contest this year. Oh, it was in all the papers; not under my own name, though. I used a nom de boulangere; I called myself Uncle Henry.

YOUNG MAN. Did you?

GRANDMA. Why not? I didn't see any reason not to. I look just as much like an old man as I do like an old woman. And you know what I called it . . . what I won for?

34

YOUNG MAN. No. What did you call it?

GRANDMA. I called it Uncle Henry's Day-Old Cake.

YOUNG MAN. That's a very nice name.

GRANDMA. And it wasn't any trouble, either. All I did was go out and get a store-bought cake, keep it around for a while, and then slip it in, unbeknownst to anybody. Simple.

YOUNG MAN. You're a very resourceful person.

GRANDMA. Pioneer stock!

YOUNG MAN. Is all this true? Do you want me to believe all this?

GRANDMA. Well, you can believe it or not; it doesn't make any difference to me. All *J* know is, Uncle Henry's Day-Old Cake won me twenty-five thousand smackerolas.

YOUNG MAN. Twenty-five thou . . .

GRANDMA. Right on the old loggerhead. Now; how do you like them apples?

YOUNG MAN. Love 'em.

GRANDMA. I thought you'd be impressed.

YOUNG MAN. Money talks.

GRANDMA. (*Pause, then, softly.*) Hey. You look familiar.

YOUNG MAN. Hm? Pardon?

GRANDMA. (*Rising and crossing* D. L., *sits* L. *chair.*) I said, you look familiar.

YOUNG MAN. Well, I've done some modeling.

GRANDMA. No; no. I don't mean that. You look familiar.

YOUNG MAN. Well, I'm a type.

GRANDMA. Yup; you sure are. Why do you say you'd do anything for money . . . if you don't mind my being nosey?

YOUNG MAN. (*Rising.*) No, no. It's part of the interview. I'll be happy to tell you. It's that I have no talents at all, except what you see . . . my person; my body, my face. In every other way I am incomplete, and I must therefore . . . compensate.

GRANDMA. What do you mean, incomplete? You look pretty complete to me.

YOUNG MAN. (*Crossing to Grandma.*) I think I can explain it to you, partially because you're very old, and very old people have perceptions they keep to themselves, because if they expose them to other people . . . well, you know what ridicule and neglect are.

GRANDMA. I do, child, I do.

YOUNG MAN. Then listen. My mother died the night that I was born, and I never knew my father; I doubt my mother did. But, I wasn't alone, because lying with me . . . in the placenta . . . there was someone else . . . my brother . . . my twin.

GRANDMA. Oh, my child.

YOUNG MAN. We were identical twins . . . he and I . . . not fraternal . . . identical; we were derived from the same ovum; and in *this*, in that we were twins not from separate ova, but from the same one, we had a kinship such as you can not imagine. We . . . we felt each other breathe . . . his heartbeats thundered in my temples . . . mine in his . . . our stomachs ached and we cried for feeding at the same time . . . are you old enough to understand?

GRANDMA. I think so, child; I think I'm nearly old enough.

YOUNG MAN. I hope so. But we were separated when we were still very young, my brother, my twin and I . . . inasmuch as you can separate one being. We were torn apart . . . thrown to opposite ends of the continent. I don't know what became of my brother . . . to the rest of myself . . . except that, from time to time, in the years that have passed, I have suffered losses . . . that I can't explain. A fall from grace . . . a departure of innocence . . . loss . . . loss. How can I put it to you? All right; like this: once . . . , it was as if all at once my heart . . . became numb . . . almost as though I . . . almost as though . . . just like that . . . it had been wrenched from my body . . . and from that time I have been unable to love. Once . . . I was asleep at the time . . . I awoke, and my eyes were burning. And since that time I have been unable to see anything, *anything*, with pity, with affection . . . with anything but . . . cool disinterest. And my groin . . . even there . . . since one time . . . one specific agony . . . since then I have not been able to *love* anyone with my body. And even my hands. . . . I can not touch another person and feel love. And there is more . . . there are more losses, but it all comes down to this; I no longer have the capacity to feel anything. I have no emotions, I have been drained; torn asunder . . . disemboweled. I have, now, only my person . . . my body . . . my face. I use what I have. . . . I let people love me. . . . I accept the syntax around me, for, while I know I cannot relate. . . . I know I must

36

be related to. I let people love me. . . . I let people touch me. . . . I let them draw pleasure from my groin . . . from my presence . . . from the fact of me . . . but, that is all it comes to. As I told you; I am incomplete. . . . I can feel nothing. I can feel nothing. (*Sits chair* L.) And so . . . here I am . . . as you see me . . . I am . . . but this . . . what you see. And it will always be thus.

GRANDMA. Oh, my child; my child. (*Long pause, then rises and crosses to him.*) I was mistaken . . . before. I don't know you from somewhere, but I knew . . . once . . . someone very much like you . . . or, very much as perhaps you were.

YOUNG MAN. (*Rises.*) Be careful; be very careful. What I have told you may not be true. In my profession. . . .

GRANDMA. Shhhhhhhhhh. (*The Young Man bows his head, in acquiescence.*) Someone . . . to be more precise . . . who might have turned out to be very much like you might have turned out to be. And . . . unless I'm terribly mistaken . . . you've found yourself a job.

YOUNG MAN. What are my duties?

MRS. BARKER. (*Off-stage.*) Yoo-hoo! Yoo-hoo!

GRANDMA. Oh-oh. You'll . . . you'll have to play it by ear, my dear . . . unless I get a chance to talk to you again. I've got to go into my act now. (*Crosses up to* L. *arch.*)

YOUNG MAN. But, I . . .

GRANDMA. Yoo-hoo!

MRS. BARKER. (*Coming through the archway.*) Yoo-hoo . . . oh, there you are, Grandma. I'm glad to see somebody; I can't find Mommy or Daddy. (*Double takes.*) Well, who's this?

GRANDMA. This? Well . . . un . . . oh, this is the . . . un . . . the van man. That's who it is; the van man.

MRS. BARKER. So! It's true! They *did* call the van man. They *are* having you carted away.

GRANDMA. (*Shrugging.*) Well, you know. It figures.

MRS. BARKER. (*To Young Man.*) How dare you cart this poor old woman away!

YOUNG MAN. (*After a quick look at Grandma, who nods.*) I do what I'm paid to do. I don't ask questions.

MRS. BARKER. (*Brief pause.*) Oh. (*Pause.*) Well, you're quite right, of course, and I shouldn't meddle.

37

GRANDMA. (*To the Young Man.*) Dear, will you take my things out to the van? (*She points to the boxes.*)

YOUNG MAN. (*After only the briefest hesitation.*) Why, certainly.

GRANDMA. (*As the Young Man takes up half the boxes, exits by the front door.*) Isn't that a nice young van man?

MRS. BARKER. (*Shaking her head in disbelief, watching the Young Man exit and crossing to arch R.*) Unh-hunh . . . some things have changed for the better. I remember when I had my mother carted off, the van man who came for her wasn't anything near as nice as this one.

GRANDMA. Oh, did you have your mother carted off, too?

MRS. BARKER. (*Cheerfully.*) Why, certainly! Didn't you?

GRANDMA. (*Puzzling.*) No. . . . No, I didn't. At least, I can't remember. (*Now back to business.*) Listen, dear; I got to talk to you for a second. (*Pulling Mrs. Barker away from arch.*)

MRS. BARKER. Why, certainly, Grandma.

GRANDMA. Now, listen.

MRS. BARKER. Yes, Grandma. Yes.

GRANDMA. Now, listen carefully. You got this dilemma here with Mommy and Daddy. . . .

MRS. BARKER. Yes! I wonder where they've gone to.

GRANDMA. They'll be back in. Now, listen!

MRS. BARKER. Oh, I'm sorry.

GRANDMA. Now, you got this dilemma here with Mommy and Daddy, and I think I got the way out for you. (*The Young Man reenters the front door.*) Will you take the rest of my things out now, dear? (*To Mrs. Barker, while the Young Man takes the rest of the boxes, exits by the front door again.*) Fine; now listen, dear. (*She begins to whisper in Mrs. Barker's ear. Mrs. Barker follows Young Man to arch R., Grandma with her, still whispering.*)

MRS. BARKER. Oh! Oh! Oh! I don't think I could . . . do you really think I could? Well, why not? What a wonderful idea . . . what an absolutely wonderful idea!

GRANDMA. Well, yes, I thought it was.

MRS. BARKER. And you so old!

GRANDMA. Heh, heh, heh.

MRS. BARKER. Well, I think it's absolutely marvelous, anyway. (*Crossing L. to arch.*) I'm going to find Mommy and Daddy right now.

GRANDMA. Good. You do that.

MRS. BARKER. Well, now. I think I will say goodbye. I can't thank you enough. (*She starts to exit through the archway.*)

GRANDMA. You're welcome. Say it!

MRS. BARKER. Huh. What?

GRANDMA. Say goodbye.

MRS. BARKER. Oh, Goodbye. (*She exits.*) Mommy! I say Mommy! Daddy!

GRANDMA. Goodbye. (*By herself now, she looks about.*) Ah, me. (*Shakes her head.*) Ah, me. (*Sits chair L. Takes in the room.*) Goodbye. (*The Young Man re-enters.*) Oh, hello there.

YOUNG MAN. All the boxes are outside. (*Sits on sofa.*)

GRANDMA. (*A little sadly.*) I don't know why I bother to take them with me. They don't have much in them . . . some old letters, a couple of regrets, Pekinese . . . blind at that . . . the television . . . my Sunday teeth . . . eighty-six years of living . . . some sounds . . . a few images, a little garbled by now . . . and, well, (*She shrugs.*) you know . . . the things one accumulates. (*Rises.*)

YOUNG MAN. (*Rising.*) Can I get you . . . a cab, or something?

GRANDMA. Oh, no, dear . . . thank you just the same. (*Crossing to arch R.*) I'll take it from here.

YOUNG MAN. And what shall I do now?

GRANDMA. Oh, you stay here, dear. It will all become clear to you. It will be explained. You'll understand.

YOUNG MAN. Very well.

GRANDMA. (*After one more look about.*) Well. . . .

YOUNG MAN. (*Crossing to Grandma.*) Let me see you to the elevator.

GRANDMA. Oh . . . that *would* be nice dear. (*They both exit, by the front door slowly. Enter Mrs. Barker, followed by Mommy and Daddy, L.*)

MRS. BARKER. (*Crossing R., gets her dress and starts putting it on.*) . . . and I'm happy to tell you that the whole thing's settled. Just like that.

MOMMY. Oh, we're so glad. We were afraid there might be a problem, what with delays, and all.

DADDY. (*Sits chair L.*) Yes, we're very relieved.

MRS. BARKER. Well, now. That's what professional women are for.

MOMMY. (*Looking around room.*) Why . . . where's Grandma? Grandma's not here! (*Grandma enters far* D. R., *secretively.*) Where's Grandma? And look! The boxes are gone too. Grandma's gone, and so are the boxes. She's taken off, and she's stolen something! Daddy!

MRS. BARKER. Why, Mommy, the van man was here.

MOMMY. (*Startled.*) The what?

MRS. BARKER. The van man. The van man was here.

MOMMY. (*Shakes her head.*) No, that's impossible.

MRS. BARKER. Why, I saw him with my own two eyes.

MOMMY. (*Crossing* c. *Near tears.*) No, no, that's impossible. No. There's no such thing as the van man. There is no van man. We . . . we made him up. Grandma? Grandma?

DADDY. (*Moving to Mommy and seating her in chair* L.) There, there, now.

MOMMY. Oh, Daddy . . . where's Grandma?

DADDY. There, there, now.

GRANDMA. (*To the audience.*) I want to watch this. (*Mrs. Barker tip-toes to the front door, and motions to Young Man who enters.*)

MRS. BARKER. Surprise! Surprise! Here we are!

MOMMY. What? What?

DADDY. Hm? What?

MOMMY. (*Her tears merely sniffles now.*) What surprise?

MRS. BARKER. (*Pushing Young Man* c.) Why, I told you. The surprise I told you about.

DADDY. (*Turns and sees Young Man.*) You . . . you know, Mommy.

MOMMY. Sur . . . prise?

DADDY. (*Urging her to cheerfulness.*) You remember, Mommy; why we asked . . . uh . . . what's-her-name to come here?

MRS. BARKER. Mrs. Barker, if you don't mind.

DADDY. Yes. Mommy, you remember now? About the bumble . . . about wanting satisfaction?

MOMMY. (*Sees Young Man. Her sorrow turning into delight.*) Yes. Why, yes! Of course! (*Rises and crosses to Young Man.*) Yes! Oh, how wonderful!

MRS. BARKER. (*To the Young Man.*) This is Mommy.

YOUNG MAN. How . . do you do.

MRS. BARKER. (*Stage whisper.*) Her name is Mommy.

YOUNG MAN. How . . . how do you do, Mommy.

MOMMY. Well! Hello there!

MRS. BARKER. (*To the Young Man.*) And that is Daddy.

YOUNG MAN. (*Crossing with hand outstretched out to Daddy, who backs off* D. L.) How do you do.

DADDY. How do you do.

MOMMY. (*Pulling Young Man* C. *Herself again, circling the Young Man, feeling his arm, poking him.*) Yes, Sir! Now this is more like it Yes, Siree! Now this is a great deal more like it! Daddy? Come see. Come see if this isn't a great deal more like it.

DADDY. I . . . I can see from here, Mommy. It does look a great deal more like it.

MOMMY. Yes, Sir. Yes, Siree! Mrs. Barker, I don't know *how* to thank you.

MRS. BARKER. Oh, don't worry about that. I'll send you a bill in the mail. (*Starts to leave, crossing to arch* R.)

MOMMY. What this really calls for is a celebration. It calls for a drink.

MRS. BARKER. (*Comes back in to* R. *chair.*) Oh, what a nice idea.

MOMMY. There's some sauterne in the kitchen.

YOUNG MAN. I'll go.

MOMMY. Will you? Oh, how nice. (*Showing him to arch* L.) The kitchen's through the archway there. (*As the Young Man exits . . . to Mrs. Barker.*) He's very nice. Really top notch; much better than the other one.

MRS. BARKER. I'm glad you're pleased. And I'm glad everything's all straightened out.

MOMMY. (*Crossing to Mrs. Barker.*) Well, at least we know why we sent for you. We're glad that's cleared up. By the way, what's his name?

MRS. BARKER. Ha! Call him whatever you like. He's yours. Call him what you called the other one.

MOMMY. Daddy? What did we call the other one?

DADDY. (*Puzzles.*) Why. . . .

YOUNG MAN. (*Re-entering with a tray, on which are five glasses.*) Here we are! (*Crosses* C. *to Mommy.*)

MOMMY. Hooray! Hooray!

MRS. BARKER. Oh, good!

MOMMY. (*Moving to the tray.*) So, let's . . . five glasses! Why five? There are only four of us. Why five?

YOUNG MAN. (*Catches Grandma's eye, Grandma indicates she is not there.*) Oh, I'm sorry.

MOMMY. You must learn to count. We're a wealthy family, and you must learn to count.

YOUNG MAN. I will.

MOMMY. Well, everybody take a glass. (*They do.*) And we'll drink to celebrate. To satisfaction! Who says you can't get satisfaction these days!

MRS. BARKER. What dreadful sauterne! (*Mrs. Barker sits chair R., Daddy sits chair L.*)

MOMMY. Yes isn't it. (*Taking tray and putting it on table R. of sofa. Then pulling Young Man down with her on sofa. To Young Man, her voice already a little fuzzy from the wine.*) You don't know how happy I am to see you! Yes Siree. Listen, that time we had with . . . with the other one. I'll tell you all about it some time. (*Indicates Mrs. Barker.*) After she's gone. She was responsible for all the trouble in the first place. I'll tell you all about it. (*Places his arm around her and sidles up to him a little.*) Maybe . . . maybe later tonight.

YOUNG MAN. (*Not moving away.*) Why, yes. That would be very nice.

MOMMY. (*Puzzles.*) Something familiar about you . . . you know that? (*Pulling him up to take a better look.*) I can't quite place it. . . . (*Daddy and Mrs. Barker turn to look at them as Grandma stops the scene. The lights dim to half and Mommy, Young Man, Daddy and Mrs. Barker are in tableau.*)

GRANDMA. (*To audience.*) Well, I guess that just about wraps it up. I mean, for better or worse, this is a comedy, and I don't think we'd better go any further. No, definitely not. So, let's leave things as they are right now . . . while everybody's happy . . . while everybody's got what he wants . . . or everybody's got what he thinks he wants. Goodnight, dears.

## CURTAIN

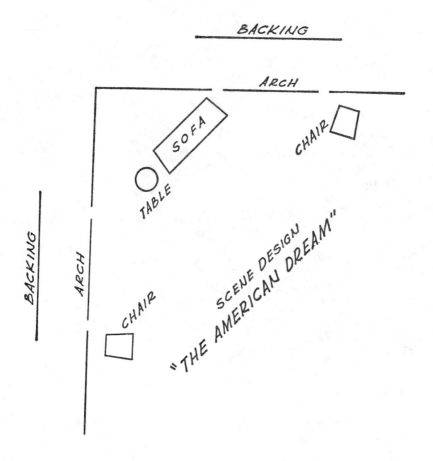

BACKING

ARCH

SOFA

CHAIR

TABLE

BACKING

ARCH

CHAIR

SCENE DESIGN
"THE AMERICAN DREAM"

## PROPERTY LIST

*Off stage* L.
Tray
5 wine glasses filled with sauterne
Boxes all sizes and shapes wrapped in heavy wrapping paper
One large box practical to sit on

*On stage*
2 empty picture frames, one hanging on flats R. and L.
1 large picture frame with 2 American flags crossed over it hanging
   on flat C. stage

*Sound*
Doorbell

# The Death of Bessie Smith

A PLAY IN EIGHT SCENES

(1959)

FIRST PERFORMANCE:

April 21, 1960

Berlin, Germany—Schlosspark Theater

FOR NED ROREM

## THE PLAYERS

BERNIE: A Negro, about forty, thin.

JACK: A dark-skinned Negro, forty-five, bulky, with a deep voice and a mustache.

THE FATHER: A thin, balding white man, about fifty-five.

THE NURSE: A southern white girl, full blown, dark or red-haired, pretty, with a wild laugh. Twenty-six.

THE ORDERLY: A light-skinned Negro, twenty-eight, clean-shaven, trim, prim.

SECOND NURSE: A southern white girl, blond, not too pretty, about thirty.

THE INTERN: A southern white man, blond, well put-together, with an amiable face; thirty.

# The Death of Bessie Smith

SCENE: *Afternoon and early evening, September 26, 1937. In and around the city of Memphis, Tennessee.*
SET: *The set for this play will vary, naturally, as stages vary—from theatre to theatre. So, the suggestions put down below, while they might serve as a useful guide, are but a general idea—what the author "sees."*

*What the author "sees" is this: The central and front area of the stage reserved for the admissions room of a hospital, for this is where the major portion of the action of the play takes place. The admissions desk and chair C., facing the audience. A door, leading outside, R.; a door, leading to further areas of the hospital, L. Very little more: a bench, perhaps, a chair or two. Running along the rear of the stage, and perhaps a bit on the sides, there should be a raised platform, on which, at various locations, against just the most minimal suggestions of sets, the other scenes of the play are performed. All of this very open, for the whole back wall of the stage is full of the sky, which will vary from scene to scene: a hot blue, a sunset, a great, red-orange-yellow sunset. Sometimes full, sometimes but a hint.*

*At the curtain, let the entire stage be dark against the sky, which is a hot blue. Music against this, for a moment or so, fading to under as the lights come up on:*

## SCENE ONE

*The corner of a barroom. Bernie seated at a table, a beer before him, with glass. Jack enters, tentatively, a beer bottle in his hand, he does not see Bernie.*

BERNIE. (*Recognizing Jack, with pleased surprise.*) Hey!
JACK. Hm?

BERNIE. Hey; Jack!

JACK. Hm? . . . What? . . . (*Recognizes him.*) Bernie!

BERNIE. What you doin' here, boy? C'mon, sit down.

JACK. Well, I'll be damned. . . .

BERNIE. C'mon, sit down, Jack.

JACK. Yeah . . . sure . . . well, I'll be damned. (*Moves over to the table, sits.*) Bernie. My God, it's hot. How you been, boy?

BERNIE. Fine; fine. What you *doin'* here?

JACK. Oh, travelin'; travelin'.

BERNIE. On the move, hunh? Boy, you are the last person I expected t'walk in that door; small world, hunh?

JACK. Yeah; yeah.

BERNIE. On the move, hunh? Where you goin'?

JACK. (*Almost, but not quite, mysterious.*) North.

BERNIE. (*Laughs.*) North! North? That's a big place, friend: north.

JACK. Yeah . . . yeah, it is that: a big place.

BERNIE. (*After a pause, laughs again.*) Well, where, boy? North *where?*

JACK. (*Coyly, proudly.*) New York.

BERNIE. New York!

JACK. Unh-hunh; unh-hunh.

BERNIE. New York, hunh? Well. What you got goin' up there?

JACK. (*Coy again.*) Oh . . . well . . . I got somethin' goin' up there. What *you* been up to, boy?

BERNIE. New York, hunh?

JACK. (*Obviously dying to tell about it.*) Unh-hunh.

BERNIE. (*Knowing it.*) Well, now, isn't that somethin'. Hey! You want a beer? You want another beer?

JACK. No, I gotta get . . . well, I don't know, I . . .

BERNIE. (*Rising from the table.*) Sure you do. Hot like this? You need a beer or two, cool you off.

JACK. (*Settling back.*) Yeah; why not? Sure, Bernie.

BERNIE. (*A dollar bill in his hand, moving off.*) I'll get us a pair. New York, hunh? What's it all about, Jack? Hunh?

JACK. (*Chuckles.*) Ah, you'd be surprised, boy; you'd be surprised. (*Lights fade on this scene, come up on another, which is:*)

# SCENE TWO

*Part of a screened-in porch, some wicker fruniture, a little the worse for wear.*

*The Nurse's Father is seated on the porch, a cane by his chair. Music, loud, from a phonograph, inside.*

FATHER. *(The music is too loud, he grips the arms of his chair, finally.)* Stop it! Stop it! Stop it! Stop it!

NURSE *(From inside.)* What? What did you say?

FATHER. STOP IT!

NURSE. *(Appearing, dressed for duty.)* I can't hear you; what do you want?

FATHER. Turn it off! Turn that goddam music off!

NURSE. Honestly, Father . . .

FATHER. Turn it off! *(The Nurse turns wearily, goes back inside. Music stops.)* Goddam nigger records. *(To Nurse, inside.)* I got a headache.

NURSE. *(Re-entering.)* What?

FATHER. I said, I got a headache; you play those goddam records all the time; blast my head off; you play those goddam nigger records full blast . . . me with a headache. . . .

NURSE. *(Wearily.)* You take your pill?

FATHER. No!

NURSE. *(Turning.)* I'll get you your pills. . . .

FATHER. I don't want 'em!

NURSE. *(Overpatiently.)* All right; then I won't get you your pills.

FATHER. *(After a pause, quietly, petulantly.)* You play those goddam records all the time. . . .

NURSE. *(Impatiently.)* I'm sorry, Father; I didn't know you had your headache.

FATHER. Don't you use that tone with me!

NURSE. *(With that tone.)* I wasn't using any tone. . . .

FATHER. Don't argue!

NURSE. I am not arguing; I don't *want* to argue; it's too hot to argue. *(Pause, then quietly.)* I don't see why a person can't play a couple of records around here without . . .

FATHER. Damn noise! That's all it is; damn noise.

NURSE. *(After a pause.)* I don't suppose you'll drive me to work.

I don't suppose, with your headache, you feel up to driving me to the hospital.

FATHER. No.

NURSE. I didn't think you would. And I suppose *you're* going to need the car, too.

FATHER. Yes.

NURSE. Yes; I figured you would. What are you going to do, Father? Are you going to sit here all afternoon on the porch, with your headache, and *watch* the car? Are you going to sit here and watch it all afternoon? You going to sit here with a shotgun and make sure the birds don't crap on it . . . or something?

FATHER. I'm going to need it.

NURSE. Yeah; sure.

FATHER. I said, I'm going to need it.

NURSE. Yeah . . . I heard you. You're going to need it.

FATHER. I am!

NURSE. Yeah; no doubt. You going to drive down to the Democratic Club, and sit around with that bunch of loafers? You going to play big politician today? Hunh?

FATHER. That's enough, now.

NURSE. You going to go down there with that bunch of bums . . . light up one of those expensive cigars, which you have no business smoking, which you can't afford, which *I* cannot afford, to put it more accurately . . . the same brand His Honor the mayor smokes . . . you going to sit down there and talk big, about how you and the mayor are like *this* . . . you going to pretend you're something more than you really are, which is nothing but . . .

FATHER. You be quiet, you!

NURSE. . . . a hanger-on . . . a flunky . . .

FATHER. YOU BE QUIET!

NURSE. (*Faster.*) Is that what you need the car for, Father, and I am going to have to take that hot, stinking bus to the hospital?

FATHER. I said, quiet! (*Pause.*) I'm sick and tired of hearing you disparage my friendship with the mayor.

NURSE. (*Contemptuous.*) Friendship!

FATHER. That's right: friendship.

NURSE. I'll tell you what I'll do: Now that we have His Honor, the mayor, as a patient . . . when I get down to the hospital . .

if I ever get there on that damn bus . . . I'll pay him a call, and I'll just *ask* him about your "friendship" with him; I'll just . . .

FATHER. Don't you go disturbing him; you hear me?

NURSE. Why, I should think the mayor would be delighted if the daughter of one of his closest friends was to . . .

FATHER. You're going to make trouble!

NURSE. (*Heavily sarcastic.*) Oh, how could I make trouble, Father?

FATHER. You be careful.

NURSE. Oh, that must be quite a friendship. Hey, I got a good idea: you could drive me down to the hospital and you could pay a visit to your good friend the mayor at the same time. Now, *that* is a good idea.

FATHER. Leave off! Just leave off!

NURSE. (*Under her breath.*) You make me sick.

FATHER. What! What was that?

NURSE. (*Very quietly.*) I said, you make me sick, Father.

FATHER. Yeah? Yeah? (*He takes his cane, raps it against the floor several times. This gesture, beginning in anger, alters, as it becomes weaker, to a helpless and pathetic flailing, eventually it subsides, the Nurse watches it all quietly.*)

NURSE. (*Tenderly.*) Are you done?

FATHER. Go away; go to work.

NURSE. I'll get you your pills before I go.

FATHER. (*Tonelessly.*) I said, I don't want them.

NURSE. I don't care whether you *want* them, or not. . . .

FATHER. I'm not one of your patients!

NURSE. Oh, and aren't I glad you're not.

FATHER. You give them better attention than you give me!

NURSE. (*Wearily.*) I don't have patients, Father; I am not a floor nurse; will you get that into your head? I am on admissions; I am on the admissions desk. You *know* that; why do you pretend otherwise?

FATHER. If you were a . . . what-do-you-call-it . . . if you were a floor nurse . . . if you *were*, you'd give your patients better attention than you give me.

NURSE. What *are* you, Father? What are you? Are you sick, or not? Are you a . . . a . . . a poor cripple, or are you planning to get yourself up out of that chair, after I go to work, and drive yourself down to the Democratic Club and sit around with that

53

bunch of loafers? Make up your mind, Father; you can't have it every which way.

FATHER. Never mind.

NURSE. You can't; you just can't.

FATHER. Never mind, now!

NURSE. (*After a pause.*) Well, I gotta get to work.

FATHER. (*Sneering.*) Why don't you get your boy friend to drive you to work?

NURSE. All right; leave off.

FATHER. Why don't you get him to come by and pick you up, hunh?

NURSE. I said, leave off!

FATHER. Or is he only interested in driving you back here at night . . . when it's nice and dark; when it's plenty dark for messing around in his car? Is that it? Why don't you bring him here and let *me* have a look at him; why don't you let me get a look at him some time?

NURSE. (*Angry.*) Well, Father . . . (*A very brief gesture at the surroundings.*) maybe it's because I don't want him to get a . . .

FATHER. I hear you; I hear you at night; I hear you gigglin' and carrying on out there in his car; I hear you!

NURSE. (*Loud, to cover the sound of his voice.*) I'm going, Father.

FATHER. All right; get along, then; get on!

NURSE. You're damned right!

FATHER. Go on! Go! (*The Nurse regards him for a moment, turns, exits.*) And don't stay out there all night in his car, when you get back. You hear me? (*Pause.*) You hear me? (*Lights fade on this scene, come up on:*)

## SCENE THREE

*A bare area. Jack enters, addresses his remarks off stage and to an invisible mirror on an invisible dresser. Music under this scene, as though coming from a distance.*

JACK. Hey . . . Bessie! C'mon, now. Hey . . . honey? Get your butt out of bed . . . wake up. C'mon; the goddam afternoon's half gone; we gotta get movin'. Hey . . . I called that son-of-a-bitch in New York . . . *I* told him, all right. I told him what you said. Wake up, baby, we gotta get out of this dump; I gotta get you to Memphis 'fore seven o'clock . . . and then . . . POW! . . . *we* are headin' straight north. Here we come; NEW YORK. I told that bastard . . . I said: Look, **you** don't have no exclusive rights on Bessie . . . nobody's got 'em . . . Bessie is doin' you a favor . . . she's doin' you a goddam favor. She don't *have* to sing for you. I said: Bessie's tired . . . she don't wanna travel now. An' he said: You don't *wanna* back out of this . . . Bessie told me *herself* . . . and I said: Look . . . don't worry yourself . . . Bessie said she'd cut more sides for you . . . she will . . . she'll make all the goddam new records you want. . . . What I mean to say *is*, just don't you get any ideas about havin' exclusive rights . . . because nobody's got 'em. (*Giggles.*) I told him you was free as a bird, honey. Free as a goddam bird. (*Looks in at her, shakes his head.*) Some bird! I been downstairs to check us out. I go downstairs to check us out, and I run into a friend of mine . . . and we sit in the bar and have a few, and he says: What're *you* doin' now; what're you doin' in this crummy hotel? And I say: I am cartin' a bird around with me. I'm cartin' her north; I got a fat lady upstairs; she is sleepin' off last night. An' he says: You always got *some* fat lady upstairs, somewhere; boy, I never seen it fail. An' I say: This ain't just no plain fat lady I got upstairs . . . this is a celebrity, boy . . . this is a rich old fat singin' lady . . . an' he laughed an' he said: Boy, who you got up there? I say: You guess. An' he says: C'mon . . . I can't guess. An' I told him . . . I am travelin' with Miss Bessie Smith. An' he looked at me, an' he said, real quiet: Jesus, boy, are you travelin' with Bessie? An' I said . . . an' real proud: You're damn right I'm travelin' with Bessie. An' he wants to meet you; so you get your big self out of bed; we're goin' to go downstairs, 'cause I wanna show you off. C'mon, now; I mean I *gotta* show you off. 'Cause then he said: "Whatever *happened* to Bessie? An' I said: What do you mean, whatever happened to Bessie? She's right upstairs. An' he said: I mean, what's she been doin' the past four-five years? There was a time there, boy, Chicago an' all, New York, she was the hottest goddam thing goin'. Is she still singin'? YOU HEAR THAT? That's what he said: Is she still singin'? An' I said . . . I said, you been tired . . . you been restin'. You ain't been forgotten, honey, but they are askin' questions. SO YOU GET UP! We're drivin' north tonight, an' when you get in New York . . . *you* show 'em where you been. Honey, you're gonna go back on top again . . . I mean it . . . you *are*. I'm gonna get you up to New York. 'Cause you gotta make that date. I mean, sure, baby, you're free as a goddam bird, an' I did tell that son-of-a-bitch he don't have exclusive rights on you . . . but, honey . . . he *is* interested . . . an' you gotta hustle for it now. You do; 'cause if you don't do *somethin'*, people are gonna stop askin' where you been the past four-five years . . . they're gonna stop askin' anything at all! You hear? An' if I say downstairs you're rich . . . that don't make it so, Bessie. No more, honey. You gotta make this goddam trip . . . you gotta get goin' again. (*Pleading.*) Baby? Honey? You know I'm not lyin' to you. C'mon now; get up. We go downstairs to the bar an' have a few . . . see my friend . . . an' then we'll get in that car . . . and *go*. 'Cause it's gettin' late, honey . . . it's gettin' awful late. (*Brighter.*) Hey! You awake? (*Moving to the wings.*) Well, c'mon, then, Bessie . . . let's get up. We're goin' north again! (*The lights fade on this scene. Music. The sunset is predominant.*)

JACK'S VOICE. Ha ha; thanks; thanks a lot. (*Car door slams. Car motor starts.*) O.K.; here we go; we're on our way. (*Sound of car motor gunning, car moving off, fading. The sunset dims again. Music, fading, as the lights come up on:*)

## SCENE FOUR

*The admissions room of the hospital. The Nurse is at her desk, the Orderly stands to one side.*

ORDERLY. The mayor of Memphis! I went into his room and there he was; the mayor of Memphis. Lying right there, flat on his belly . . . a cigar in his mouth . . . an unlit cigar stuck in his mouth, chewing on it, chewing on a big, unlit cigar . . . shuffling a lot of papers in his hands, a pillow shoved up under his chest to give him some freedom for all those papers . . . and I came in, and I said: Good afternoon, Your Honor . . . and he swung his face 'round and he looked at me and he shouted: My ass hurts, you get the hell out of here!

56

NURSE. (*Laughs freely.*) His Honor has got his ass in a sling, and that's for sure.

ORDERLY. And I got out; I left very quickly; I closed the door fast.

NURSE. The mayor and his hemorrhoids . . . the mayor's late hemorrhoids . . . are a matter of deep concern to this institution, for the mayor built this hospital; the mayor is here with his ass in a sling, and the seat of government is now in Room 206 . . . so you be nice and respectful. (*Laughs.*) There is a man two rooms down who walked in here last night after you went off . . . that man walked in here with his hands over his gut to keep his insides from spilling right out on this desk . . .

ORDERLY. I heard. . . .

NURSE. . . . and that man may live, or he may not live, and the wagers are heavy that he will not live . . . but we are not one bit more concerned for that man than we are for His Honor . . . no sir.

ORDERLY. (*Chuckling.*) I like your contempt.

NURSE. You what? You like my *contempt*, do you? Well now, don't misunderstand me. Just what do you think I meant? What have you got it in your mind that I was saying?

ORDERLY. Why, it's a matter of proportion. Surely you don't *condone* the fact that the mayor and his piles, and that poor man lying up there . . . ?

NURSE. *Condone!* Will you listen to that: condone! My! Aren't you the educated one! What . . . what does that word mean, boy? That word condone. Hunh? You do talk some, don't you? You have a great deal to learn. Now it's true that the poor man lying up there with his guts coming out could be a nigger for all the attention he'd get if His Honor should start shouting for something . . . he could be on the operating table . . . and they'd drop his insides right on the floor and come running if the mayor should want his cigar lit. . . . But that is the way things *are.* Those are facts. You had better acquaint yourself with some realities.

ORDERLY. I know . . . I know the mayor is an important man. He *is* impressive . . . even lying on his belly like he is. . . . I'd like to get to talk to him.

NURSE. Don't you know it! TALK to him! Talk to the mayor? What for?

ORDERLY. I've told you. I've told you I don't intend to stay here carrying crap pans and washing out the operating theatre until I have a . . . a long gray beard . . . I'm . . . I'm going beyond that.

NURSE. (*Patronizing.*) Sure.

ORDERLY. I've told you . . . I'm going beyond that. This . . .

NURSE. (*Shakes her head in amused disbelief.*) Oh, my. Listen . . . you should count yourself lucky, boy. Just what do you think is going to happen to you? Is His Honor, the mayor, going to rise up out of his sickbed and take a personal interest in you? Write a letter to the President, maybe? And is Mr. Roosevelt going to send his wife, Lady Eleanor, down here after you? Or is it in your plans that you are going to be handed a big fat scholarship somewhere to the north of Johns Hopkins? Boy, you just don't know! I'll tell you something . . . you are lucky as you are. Whatever do you expect?

ORDERLY. What's been promised. . . . Nothing more. Just that.

NURSE. Promised! Promised? Oh, boy, I'll tell you about promises. Don't you know yet that everything is promises . . . and that is all there is to it? Promises . . . nothing more! I am personally sick of promises. Would you like to hear a little poem? Would you like me to recite some verse for you? Here is a little poem: "You kiss the niggers and I'll kiss the Jews and we'll stay in the White House as long as we choose." And that . . . according to what I am told . . . that is what Mr. and Mrs. Roosevelt sit at the breakfast table and sing to each other over their orange juice, right in the White House. Promises, boy! Promises . . . and that is what they are going to stay.

ORDERLY. There are *some* people who believe in more than promises. . . .

NURSE. Hunh?

ORDERLY. (*Cautious now.*) I say, there are some people who believe in more than promises; there are some people who believe in action.

NURSE. What's that? What did you say?

ORDERLY. Action . . . ac— . . . Never mind.

NURSE. (*Her eyes narrow.*) No . . . no, go on now . . . action? What kind of action do you mean?

ORDERLY. I don't *mean* anything . . . all I said was . . .

NURSE. I heard you. You know . . . I know what you been

58

doing. You been listening to the great white doctor again . . .
that big, good-looking blond intern you *admire* so much because
he is so liberal-thinking, eh? My suitor? (*Laughs.*) My suitor
. . . my very own white knight, who is wasting his time patching
up decent folk right here when there is dying going on in Spain.
(*Exaggerated.*) Oh, there is dying in Spain. And he is held here!
That's who you have been listening to.

ORDERLY. I don't mean that. . . . I don't pay any attention
. . . (*Weakly.*) to that kind of talk. I do my job here . . . I
try to keep . . .

NURSE. (*Contemptuous.*) You try to keep yourself on the good
side of everybody, don't you, boy? You stand there and you
nod your kinky little´ head and say yes'm, yes'm, at everything
I say, and then when he's here you go off in a corner and you
get him and you sympathize with him . . . you get him to
tell you about . . . promises! . . . and . . . and . . . action!
. . . I'll tell you right now, he's going to get himself into trouble
. . . and you're helping him right along.

ORDERLY. No, now. I don't . . .

NURSE. (*With some disgust.*) All that talk of his! Action! I
know all what he talks about . . . like about that bunch of
radicals came through here last spring . . . causing that rioting
. . . that arson! Stuff like that. Didn't . . . didn't you have
someone get banged up in that?

ORDERLY. (*Contained.*) My uncle got run down by a lorry full
of state police . . .

NURSE. . . . which the Governor called out because of the rioting . . . and that arson! Action! That was a fine bunch of
action. Is that what you mean? Is that what you get him off in
a corner and get him to talk about . . . and pretend you're interested? Listen, boy . . . if you're going to get yourself in
with those folks, you'd better . . .

ORDERLY. (*Quickly.*) I'm not mixed up with any folks . . .
honestly . . . I'm not. I just want to . . .

NURSE. I'll tell you what you just want. . . . I'll tell you what
you just want if you have any mind to keep this good job you've
got. . . . You just shut your ears . . . and you keep that
mouth closed tight, too. All this talk about what you are going
to go beyond! You keep walking a real tight line here, and . . .
and at night . . . (*She begins to giggle*) . . . and at night, if

you want to, on your own time . . . at night you keep right on putting that bleach on your hands and your neck and your face . . .

ORDERLY. I do no such thing!

NURSE. (*In full laughter.*) . . . and you keep right on bleaching away . . . b-l-e-a-c-h-i-n-g a-w-a-y . . . but you do that on your own time . . . you can do all that on your own time.

ORDERLY. (*Pleading.*) I do no such thing!

NURSE. The hell you don't! You are such a . . .

ORDERLY. That kind of talk is very . . .

NURSE. . . . you are so mixed up! You are going to be one funny sight. You, over there in a corner playing up to him . . . well, boy, you are going to be one funny sight come the millennium. . . . The great black mob marching down the street, banners in the air . . . that great black mob . . . and you right there in the middle, your bleached-out, snowy-white face in the middle of the pack like that . . . (*She breaks down in laughter.*) . . . oh . . . oh, my . . . oh. I tell you, that will be quite a sight.

ORDERLY. (*Plaintive.*) I wish you'd stop that.

NURSE. Quite a sight.

ORDERLY. I wish you wouldn't make fun of me . . . I don't give you any cause.

NURSE. Oh, my . . . oh, I *am* sorry . . . I am *so* sorry.

ORDERLY. I don't think I give you any cause. . . .

NURSE. You don't, eh?

ORDERLY. No.

NURSE. Well . . . you *are* a true little gentleman, that's for sure . . . you *are* polite . . . and deferential . . . and you are a genuine little ass-licker, if I ever saw one. Tell me, boy . . .

ORDERLY. (*Stiffening a little.*) There is no need . . .

NURSE. (*Maliciously solicitous.*) Tell me, boy . . . is it true that you have Uncle Tom'd yourself right out of the bosom of your family . . . right out of your circle of acquaintances? Is it true, young man, that you are now an inhabitant of no-man's-land, on the one side shunned and disowned by your brethren, and on the other an object of contempt and derision to your betters? Is that your problem, son?

ORDERLY. You . . . you shouldn't do that. I . . . work hard . . . I try to advance myself . . . I give nobody trouble.

NURSE. I'll tell you what you do. . . . You go north, boy . . .

you go up to New York City, where nobody's any better than
anybody else . . . get up north, boy. (*Abrupt change of tone.*)
But before you do anything like that, you run on downstairs and
get me a pack of cigarettes.
ORDERLY. (*Pauses. Is about to speak, thinks better of it, moves
off to door, L.*) Yes'm. (*Exits.*)
NURSE. (*Watches him leave. After he is gone, shakes her head,
laughs, parodies him.*) Yes'm . . . yes'm . . . ha, ha, ha! You
white niggers kill me. (*She picks up her desk phone, dials a
number, as the lights come up on:*)

## SCENE FIVE

*Which is both the hospital set of the preceding scene
and, as well, on the raised platform, another admissions
desk of another hospital. The desk is empty. The phone
rings, twice. The Second Nurse comes in, slowly, filing
her nails, maybe.*

SECOND NURSE. (*Lazily answering the phone.*) Mercy Hospi-
tal.
NURSE. Mercy Hospital! Mercy, indeed, you away from your
desk all the time. *Some* hospitals are run better than *others, some*
nurses stay at their posts.
SECOND NURSE. (*Bored.*) Oh, hi. What do you want?
NURSE. I don't *want* anything. . . .
SECOND NURSE. (*Pause.*) Oh. Well, what did you call for?
NURSE. I didn't call *for* anything. I (*Shrugs.*) just called.
SECOND NURSE. Oh. (*The lights dim a little on the two nurses.
Music. Car sounds up.*)
JACK'S VOICE. (*Laughs.*) I tell you, honey, he didn't like that.
No, sir, he didn't. You comfortable, honey. Hunh? You just lean
back and enjoy the ride, baby; we're makin' good time. Yes, we
are makin' . . . WATCH OUT! WATCH . . . (*Sound of
crash. . . . Silence.*) Honey . . . baby . . . we have crashed
. . . you all right? . . . BESSIE! BESSIE! (*Music up again,
fading as the lights come up full again on the two nurses.*)
NURSE. . . . and, what else? Oh, yeah; *we* have got the mayor
here.
SECOND NURSE. That's nice. What's he doin'?

NURSE. He isn't *doin'* anything; he is a patient here.
SECOND NURSE. Oh. Well, *we* had the mayor's wife *here* . . .
last April.
NURSE. Unh-hunh. Well, *we* got the mayor *here*, now.
SECOND NURSE. (*Very bored.*) Unh-hunh. Well, that's nice.
NURSE. (*Turns, sees the Intern entering.*) Oh, lover-boy just
walked in; I'll call you later, hunh?
SECOND NURSE. Unh-hunh. (*They both hang up. The lights
fade on the Second Nurse.*)

## SCENE SIX

NURSE. Well, how is the Great White Doctor this evening?
INTERN. (*Irritable.*) Oh . . . drop it.
NURSE. Oh, my . . . where is your cheerful demeanor this
evening, Doctor?
INTERN. (*Smiling in spite of himself.*) How do you do it?
How do you manage to just dismiss things from your mind? How
can you say a . . . cheerful hello to someone . . . dismissing
from your mind . . . excusing yourself for the vile things you
have said the evening before?
NURSE. (*Lightly.*) I said nothing vile. I put you in your place . . .
that's all. I . . . I merely put you in your place . . . as I have
done before . . . and as I shall do again.
INTERN. (*Is about to say something, thinks better of it, sighs.*)
Never mind . . . forget about it . . . Did you *see* the sunset?
NURSE. (*Mimicking.*) No, I didn't *see* the sunset. *What* is it
doing?
INTERN. (*Amused. Puts it on heavily.*) The west is burning . . .
fire has enveloped fully half of the continent . . . the . . . the
fingers of the flame stretch upward to the stars . . . and . . .
and there is a monstrous burning circumference hanging on the
edge of the world.
NURSE. (*Laughs.*) Oh, my . . . oh, my.
INTERN. (*Serious.*) It's a truly beautiful sight. Go out and have
a look.
NURSE. (*Coquettish.*) Oh, Doctor, I am chained to my desk of
pain, so I must rely on you. . . . Talk the sunset to me, you
. . . you monstrous burning intern hanging on the edge of my
circumference . . . ha, ha, ha.

INTERN. (*Leans toward her.*) When?

NURSE. When?

INTERN. (*Lightly.*) When . . . when are you going to let me nearer, woman?

NURSE. Oh, my!

INTERN. Here am I . . . here am I tangential, while all the while I would serve more nobly as a radiant, not outward from, but reversed, plunging straight to your lovely vortex.

NURSE. (*Laughs.*) Oh, la! You must keep your mind off my lovely vortex . . . you just remain . . . uh . . . tangential.

INTERN. (*Mock despair.*) How is a man to fulfill himself? Here I offer you love . . . consider the word . . . love. . . . Here I offer you my love, my self . . . my bored bed . . .

NURSE. I note your offer . . . your offer is noted. (*Holds out a clip board.*) Here . . . do you want your reports?

INTERN. No . . . I don't want my reports. Give them here. (*Takes the clip board.*)

NURSE. And while you're here with your hot breath on me, hand me a cigarette. I sent the nigger down for a pack. I ran out. (*He gives her a cigarette.*) Match?

INTERN. Go light it on the sunset. (*Tosses match to her.*) He says you owe him for three packs.

NURSE. (*Lights her cigarette.*) Your bored bed . . . indeed.

INTERN. Ma'am . . . the heart yearns, the body burns . . .

NURSE. And I haven't time for *interns.*

INTERN. . . . the heart yearns, the body burns . . . and I haven't time . . . Oh, I don't know . . . the things you women can do to art. (*More intimate, but still light.*) Have you told your father, yet? Have you told your father that I am hopelessly in love with you? Have you told him that at night the sheets of my bed are like a tent, poled center-upward in my love for you?

NURSE. (*Wry.*) I'll tell him . . . I'll tell my father just that . . . just what you said . . . and he'll be down here after you for talking to a young lady like that! Really!

INTERN. My God! I forgot myself! A cloistered maiden in whose house trousers are never mentioned . . . in which flies, I am sure, are referred to only as winged bugs. Here I thought I was talking to someone, to a certain young nurse, whose collection of anatomical jokes for all occasions . . .

NURSE. (*Giggles.*) Oh, you be still, now. (*Lofty.*) Besides, just because I play coarse and flip around here . . . to keep my place with the rest of you . . . don't you think for a minute that I relish this turn to the particular from the general. . . . If you don't mind, we'll just cease this talk.

INTERN. (*Half sung.*) I'm always in tumescence for you. You'd never guess the things I . . .

NURSE. (*Blush-giggle.*) Now stop that! Really, I mean it!

INTERN. Then marry me, woman. If nothing else, marry me.

NURSE. Don't, now.

INTERN. (*Joking and serious at the same time.*) Marry me.

NURSE. (*Matter-of-fact, but not unkindly.*) I am sick of this talk. My poor father may have some funny ideas; he may be having a pretty hard time reconciling himself to things as they are. But not me! Forty-six dollars a month! Isn't that right? Isn't that what you make? Forty-six dollars a month! Boy, you can't afford even to think about marrying. You can't afford marriage. . . . Best you can afford is lust. That's the best you can afford.

INTERN. (*Scathing.*) Oh . . . gentle woman . . . nineteenth-century lady out of place in this vulgar time . . . maiden versed in petit point and murmured talk of the weather . . .

NURSE. Now I mean it . . . you can cut that talk right out.

INTERN. . . . type my great-grandfather fought and died for . . . forty-six dollars a month and the best I can afford is lust! Jesus, woman!

NURSE. All right . . . you can quit making fun of me. You can quit it right this minute.

INTERN. *I*/ Making fun of *you* . . . !

NURSE. I am tired of being toyed with; I am tired of your impractical propositions. Must you dwell on what is not going to happen? Must you ask me, constantly, over and over again, the same question to which you are already aware you will get the same answer? Do you get pleasure from it? What unreasonable form of contentment do you derive from persisting in this?

INTERN. (*Lightly.*) Because I love you?

NURSE. Oh, that would help matters along; it really would . . . even if it were *true*. The economic realities would pick up their skirts, whoop, and depart before the lance-high, love-smit knight. My knight, whose real and true interest, if we come right down

64

to it, as indicated in the order of your propositions, is, and always has been, a convenient and uncomplicated bedding down.

INTERN. (*Smiling, and with great gallantry.*) I have offered to marry you.

NURSE. Yeah . . . sure . . . you have offered to marry me. The United States is chuck-full of girls who have heard that great promise—I will marry you . . . I will marry you . . . IF! If! The great promise with its great conditional attached to it. . . .

INTERN. (*Amused.*) Who are you pretending to be?

NURSE. (*Abrupt.*) What do you mean?

INTERN. (*Laughing.*) Oh, nothing.

NURSE. (*Regards him silently for a moment, then.*) Marry me! Do you know . . . do you know that nigger I sent to fetch me a pack of butts . . . do you know he is in a far better position . . . realistically, economically . . . to ask to marry me than you are? Hunh? Do you know that? That nigger! Do you know that nigger outearns you . . . and by a *lot*?

INTERN. (*Bows to her.*) I know he does . . . and I know what value you, you and your famous family, put on such things. So, I have an idea for you . . . why don't you just *ask* that nigger to marry you? 'Cause, boy, he'd never ask you! I'm sure if you told your father about it, it would give him some pause at first, because we know what type of man your father is . . . don't we? . . . But then he would think about it . . . and realize the advantages of the match . . . realistically . . . economically . . . and he would find some way to adjust his values, in consideration of your happiness, and security. . . .

NURSE. (*Flicks her still-lit cigarette at him, hard, hits him with it.*) You are disgusting!

INTERN. Damn you, bitch!

NURSE. Disgusting!

INTERN. Realistic . . . practical . . . (*A little softer, now.*) Your family is a famous *name*, but those thousand acres are *gone*, and the pillars of your house are blistered and flaking . . . (*Harder.*) Not that your family ever *had*, within human memory, a thousand acres to *go* . . . or a house with pillars in the first place. . . .

NURSE. (*Angry.*) I am fully aware of what is true and what is not true. (*Soberly.*) Go about your work and leave me be.

INTERN. (*Sweetly.*) Aw.

NURSE. I said . . . leave me be.

INTERN. (*Brushing himself.*) It is a criminal offense to set fire to interns . . . orderlies you may burn at will, unless you have other plans for them . . . but interns . . .

NURSE. . . . are a dime a dozen. (*Giggles.*) Did I burn you?

INTERN. No, you did not burn me.

NURSE. That's too bad . . . would have served you right if I had. (*Pauses, then smiles.*) I'm sorry, honey.

INTERN. (*Mock formal.*) I accept your apology . . . and I await your surrender.

NURSE. (*Laughs.*) Well, you just await it. (*A pause.*) Hey, what are you going to do about the mayor being here now?

INTERN. What am I supposed to do about it? I am on emergencies, and he is not an emergency case.

NURSE. I told you . . . I told you what you should do.

INTERN. I know . . . I should go upstairs to his room . . . I should pull up a chair, and I should sit down and I should say, How's tricks, Your Honor?

NURSE. Well, you make fun if you want to . . . but if you listen to me, you'll know you need some people *behind* you.

INTERN. Strangers!

NURSE. Strangers don't stay strangers . . . not if you don't let them. He could do something for you if he had a mind to.

INTERN. Yes he could . . . indeed, he *could* do something for me. . . . He could give me his car . . . he could make me a present of his Cord automobile. . . . That would be the finest thing any mayor ever did for a private citizen. Have you seen that car?

NURSE. Have I seen that car? Have I seen this . . . have I seen that? Cord automobiles and . . . and sunsets . . . those are . . . fine preoccupations. Is that what you think about? Huh? Driving a fine car into a fine sunset?

INTERN. (*Quietly.*) Lord knows, I'd like to get away from here.

NURSE. (*Nodding.*) I know . . . I know. Well, maybe you're going to *have* to get away from here. People are aware how dissatisfied you are . . . people have heard a lot about your . . . dissatisfactions. . . . My father has heard . . . people got wind of the way you feel about things. People here aren't good enough for your attentions. . . . Foreigners . . . a bunch of foreigners who are cutting each other up in their own business . . . that's where you'd like to be, isn't it?

INTERN. (*Quietly, intensely.*) There are over half a million people killed in that war! Do you know that? By airplanes. . . . Civilians! You misunderstand me so! I am . . . all right . . . this way. . . . My dissatisfactions . . . you call them that . . . my dissatisfactions have nothing to do with loyalties. . . . I am not concerned with politics . . . but I have a sense of urgency . . . a dislike of waste . . . stagnation . . . I am *stranded* . . . *here.* . . . My talents are not large . . . but the emergencies of the emergency ward of this second-rate hospital in this second-rate state . . . No! . . . it isn't enough. Oh, you listen to me. If I could . . . if I could bandage the arm of one person . . . if I could be over there right this minute . . . you could take the city of Memphis . . . you could take the whole state . . . and don't you forget I was born here . . . you could take the whole goddam state. . . .

NURSE. (*Hard.*) Well, I have a very good idea of how we could arrange that. I have a dandy idea. . . . We could just tell the mayor about the way you feel, and he'd be delighted to help you on your way . . . out of this hospital at the very least, and maybe out of the state! And I don't think he'd be giving you any Cord automobile as a going-away present, either. He'd set you out, all right . . . he'd set you right out on your *butt!* That's what he'd do.

INTERN. (*With a rueful half-smile.*) Yes . . . yes . . . I imagine he would. I feel lucky . . . I feel doubly fortunate, now . . . having you . . . feeling the way we do about each other.

NURSE. You are so sarcastic!

INTERN. Well, how the hell do you expect me to behave?

NURSE. Just . . . (*Laughs.*) . . . oh, boy, this is good . . . just like I told the nigger . . . you walk a straight line, and you do your job . . . (*Turns coy, here.*) . . . and . . . and unless you are kept late by some emergency more pressing than your . . . (*Smiles wryly.*) . . . "love" . . . for me . . . I may let you drive me home tonight . . . in your beat-up Chevvy.

INTERN. Woman, as always I anticipate with enormous pleasure the prospect of driving you home . . . a stop along the way . . . fifteen minutes or so of . . . of tantalizing preliminary love play ending in an infuriating and inconclusive wrestling match, during which you hiss of the . . . the liberties I should not take, and I sound the horn once or twice accidentally with my elbow . . . (*She giggles at this.*) . . . and, finally, in my beat-up car, in front of your father's beat-up house . . . a kiss of searing intensity . . . a hand in the right place . . . briefly . . . and your hasty departure within. I am looking forward to this ritual . . . as I always do.

NURSE. (*Pleased.*) Why, thank you.

INTERN. I look forward to this ritual because of how it sets me apart from other men . . .

NURSE. Aw . . .

INTERN. . . . because I am probably the only white man under sixty in two counties who has *not* had the pleasure of . . .

NURSE. LIAR! You no-account mother-grabbing son of a nigger!

INTERN. (*Laughs.*) Boy! Watch you go!

NURSE. FILTH! You are filth!

INTERN. I am honest . . . an honest man. Let me make you an honest woman.

NURSE. (*Steaming . . . her rage between her teeth.*) You have done it, boy . . . you have played around with me and you have done it. I am going to get you . . . I am going to fix you . . . I am going to see to it that you are *through* here . . . do you understand what I'm telling you?

INTERN. There is no ambiguity in your talk now, honey.

NURSE. You're damn right there isn't. (*The Orderly re-enters from L. The Nurse sees him.*) Get out of here! (*But he stands there.*) Do you hear me? You get the hell out of here! Go (*He retreats, exits, to silence.*)

INTERN. (*Chuckling.*) King of the castle. My, you *are* something.

NURSE. Did you get what I was telling you?

INTERN. Why, I heard every word . . . every sweet syllable. . . .

NURSE. You have overstepped yourself . . . and you are going to wish you hadn't. I'll get my father . . . I'll have you done with *myself*.

INTERN. (*Cautious.*) Aw, come on, now.

NURSE. I mean it.

INTERN. (*Lying badly.*) Now look . . . you don't think I meant . . .

NURSE. (*Mimicking.*) Now you don't think I meant . . .

(*Laughs broadly.*) Oh, my . . . you are the funny one. (*Her threat, now, has no fury, but is filled with quiet conviction.*) I said I'll fix you . . . and I will. You just go along with your work . . . you do your job . . . but what I said . . . you keep that burning in the back of your brain. We'll go right along, you and I, and we'll be civil . . . and it'll be as though nothing had happened . . . nothing at all. (*Laughs again.*) Honey, your neck is in the *noose* . . . and I have a whip . . . and I'll set the horse from under you . . . when it pleases me.

INTERN. (*Wryly.*) It's going to be nice around here.

NURSE. Oh, yes it is. I'm going to enjoy it . . . I really am.

INTERN. Well . . . I'll forget about driving you home tonight. . . .

NURSE. Oh, no : . . . you will *not* forget about driving me home tonight. You will drive me home *tonight* . . . you will drive me home *tonight* . . . and *tomorrow* night . . . you will see me to my *door* . . . you will be my gallant. We will have things between us a little bit the way I am told things *used* to be. You will *court* me, boy, and you will do it *right!*

INTERN. (*Stares at her for a moment.*) You impress me. No matter what else, I've got to admit that. (*The Nurse laughs wildly at this. Music. The lights on this hospital set fade, and come up on the Second Nurse, at her desk, for:*)

## SCENE SEVEN

JACK. (*Rushing in.*) Ma'am, I need help, quick!

SECOND NURSE. What d'you want here?

JACK. There has been an accident, ma'am . . . I got an injured woman outside in my car. . . .

SECOND NURSE. Yeah? Is that so? Well, you sit down and wait. . . . You go over there and sit down and wait a while.

JACK. This is an emergency! There has been an accident!

SECOND NURSE. YOU WAIT! You just sit down and wait!

JACK. This woman is badly hurt. . . .

SECOND NURSE. YOU COOL YOUR HEELS!

JACK. Ma'am . . . I got Bessie Smith out in that car there. . . .

SECOND NURSE. I DON'T CARE WHO YOU GOT OUT THERE, NIGGER. YOU COOL YOUR HEELS! (*Music up.*

*The lights fade on this scene, come up again on the main hospital scene, on the Nurse and the Intern, for:)*

## SCENE EIGHT

*(Music fades.)*

NURSE. *(Loud.)* Hey, nigger . . . nigger! *(The Orderly re-enters, L.)* Give me my cigarettes.

INTERN. I think I'll . . .

NURSE. You stay here! *(The Orderly hands the Nurse the ciga-rettes, cautious and attentive to see what is wrong.)* A person could die for a smoke, the time you take. What'd you do . . . sit downstairs in the can and rest your small, shapely feet . . . hunh?

ORDERLY. You told me to . . . go back outside . . .

NURSE. Before that! What'd you do . . . go to the cigarette *factory?* Did you take a quick run up to Winston-Salem for these?

ORDERLY. No . . . I . . .

NURSE. Skip it. *(To the Intern.)* Where? Where were you plan-ning to go?

INTERN. *(Too formal.)* I beg your pardon?

NURSE. I said . . . where did you want to go to? Were you off for coffee?

INTERN. Is that what you want? Now that you have your ciga-rettes, have you hit upon the idea of having coffee, too? Now that he is back from one errand, are you planning to send me on another?

NURSE. *(Smiling wickedly.)* Yeah . . . I think I'd like that . . . keep both of you jumping. I *would* like coffee, and I *would* like you to get it for me. So why don't you just trot right across the hall and get me some? And I like it good and hot . . . and strong . . .

INTERN. . . . and black . . . ?

NURSE. Cream! . . . and sweet . . . and in a hurry!

INTERN. I guess your wish is my command . . . hunh?

NURSE. You bet it is!

INTERN. *(Moves halfway to the door, L., then pauses.)* I just had a lovely thought . . . that maybe sometime when you are sitting there at your desk opening mail with that stiletto you

70

use for a letter opener, you might slip and tear open your arm . . . then you could come running into the emergency . . . and I could be there when you came running in, blood coming out of you like water out of a faucet . . . and I could take ahold of your arm . . . and just hold it . . . just hold it . . . and watch it flow . . . just hold on to you and watch your blood flow. . . .

NURSE. (*Grabs up the letter opener . . . holds it up.*) This? More likely between your ribs!

INTERN. (*Exiting.*) One coffee, lady.

NURSE. (*After a moment of silence, throws the letter opener back down on her desk.*) I'll take care of him. CRACK! I'll crack that whip. (*To the Orderly.*) What are you standing there for . . . hunh? You like to watch what's going on?

ORDERLY. I'm no voyeur.

NURSE. You what? You like to listen in? You take pleasure in it?

ORDERLY. I said no.

NURSE. (*Half to herself.*) I'll bet you don't. I'll take care of him . . . talking to me like that . . . I'll crack that whip. Let him just wait. (*To the Orderly, now.*) My father says that Francisco Franco is going to be victorious in that war over there . . . that he's going to win . . . and that it's just wonderful.

ORDERLY. He does?

NURSE. Yes, he does. My father says that Francisco Franco has got them licked, and that they're a bunch of radicals, anyway, and it's all to the good . . . just wonderful.

ORDERLY. Is that so?

NURSE. I've told you my father is a . . . a historian, so he isn't just anybody. His opinion counts for something special. It *still* counts for something special. He says anybody wants to go over there and get mixed up in that thing has got it coming to him . . . whatever happens.

ORDERLY. I'm sure your father is an informed man, and . . .

NURSE. What?

ORDERLY. I said . . . I said . . . I'm sure your father is an informed man, and . . . his opinion is to be respected.

NURSE. That's right, boy . . . you just jump to it and say what you think people want to hear . . . you be both sides of the coin. Did you . . . did you hear him threaten me there? Did you?

ORDERLY. Oh, now . . . I don't think . . .

NURSE. (*Steely.*) You heard him threaten me!

ORDERLY. I don't think . . .

NURSE. For such a smart boy . . . you are so dumb. I don't know what I am going to do with you. (*She is thinking of the Intern now, and her expression shows it.*) You refuse to comprehend things, and that bodes badly . . . it does. Especially considering it is all but arranged . . .

ORDERLY. What is all but arranged?

NURSE. (*A great laugh, but mirthless. She is barely under control.*) Why, don't you know, boy? Didn't you know that you and I are practically engaged?

ORDERLY. I . . . I don't . . .

NURSE. Don't you know about the economic realities? Haven't you been appraised of the way things *are?* (*She giggles.*) Our knights are gone forth into sunsets . . . behind the wheels of Cord cars . . . the acres have diminished and the paint is flaking . . . that there is a great . . . *abandonment?*

ORDERLY. (*Cautious.*) I don't understand you. . . .

NURSE. No kidding? (*Her voice shakes.*) No kidding . . . you don't understand me? Why? What's the matter, boy, don't you get the idea?

ORDERLY. (*Contained, but angry.*) I think you'd tire of riding me some day. I think you *would.* . . .

NURSE. You go up to Room 206, right now . . . you go up and tell the mayor that when his butt's better we have a marrying job for him.

ORDERLY. (*With some distaste.*) Really . . . you go much too far. . . .

NURSE. Oh, I do, do I? Well, let me tell you something . . . I am sick of it! I am *sick.* I am sick of everything in this hot, stupid, fly-ridden *world.* I am sick of the disparity between things as they are, and as they should be! I am sick of this desk . . . this uniform . . . it scratches. . . . I am sick of the sight of *you* . . . the *thought* of you makes me . . . *itch.* . . . I am sick of *him.* (*Soft now: a chant.*) I am sick of talking to people on the phone in this damn stupid hospital. . . . I am sick of the smell of Lysol . . . I could die of it. . . . I am sick of going to bed and I am sick of waking up. . . . I am tired . . . I am tired of the truth . . . and I am tired of lying about the truth . . . I am tired of my skin. . . . I WANT OUT!

ORDERLY. (*After a short pause.*) Why don't you go into emergency . . . and lie down? (*He approaches her.*)

NURSE. Keep away from me. (*At this moment the outside door bursts open* R., *and Jack plunges into the room. He is all these things: drunk, shocked, frightened. His face should be cut, but no longer bleeding. His clothes should be dirtied . . . and in some disarray. He pauses, a few steps into the room, breathing hard.*) Whoa! Hold on there, you.

ORDERLY. (*Not advancing.*) What do you want?

JACK. (*After more hard breathing, confused.*) What . . . ?

NURSE. You come banging in through that door like that? What's the matter with you? (*To the Orderly.*) Go see what's the matter with him.

ORDERLY. (*Advancing slightly.*) What do you *want*?

JACK. (*Very confused.*) What do I want . . . ?

ORDERLY. (*Backing off.*) You can't come in here like this . . . banging your way in here . . . don't you know any better?

NURSE. You drunk?

JACK. (*Taken aback by the irrelevance.*) I've been drinking . . . yes . . . all right . . . I'm drunk. (*Intense.*) I got someone outside . . .

NURSE. You stop that yelling. This is a white hospital, you.

ORDERLY. (*Nearer the Nurse.*) That's right. She's right. This is a private hospital . . . a semiprivate hospital. If you go on . . . into the city . . .

JACK. (*Shakes his head.*) No. . . .

NURSE. Now you listen to me, and you get this straight . . . (*Pauses just perceptibly, then says the word, but with no special emphasis.*) . . . nigger . . . this is a semiprivate white hospital . . .

JACK. (*Defiant.*) I don't care!

NURSE. Well, you get on. . . .

ORDERLY. (*As the Intern re-enters* L. *with two containers of coffee.*) You go on now . . . you go . . .

INTERN. What's all this about?

ORDERLY. I told him to go on into Memphis . . .

INTERN. Be quiet. (*To Jack.*) What is all this about?

JACK. Please . . . I got a woman . . .

NURSE. You been told to move on.

INTERN. You got a woman . . .

73

JACK. Outside . . . in the car. . . . There was an accident . . . there is blood. . . . Her arm . . .

INTERN. (*After thinking for a moment, looking at the Nurse, moves toward the outside door.*) All right . . . we'll go see. (*To the Orderly, who hangs back.*) Come on, you . . . let's go.

ORDERLY. (*Looks to the Nurse.*) We told him to go on into Memphis.

NURSE. (*To the Intern, her eyes narrowing.*) Don't you go out there!

INTERN. (*Ignoring her, to the Orderly.*) You heard me . . . come on!

NURSE. (*Strong.*) I told you . . . DON'T GO OUT THERE!

INTERN. (*Softly, sadly.*) Honey . . . you going to fix me? You going to have the mayor throw me out of here on my butt? Or are you going to arrange it in Washington to have me *deported*? What are you going to do . . . hunh?

NURSE. (*Between her teeth.*) Don't go out there. . . .

INTERN. Well, honey, whatever it is you're going to do . . . it might as well be now as any other time. (*He and the Orderly move to the outside door, R.*)

NURSE. (*Half angry, half plaintive, as they exit.*) Don't go! (*After they exit.*) I warn you! I *will* fix you. You go out that door . . . you're through here. (*Jack moves to a vacant area near the bench L. The Nurse lights a cigarette.*) I told you I'd fix you . . . I'll fix you. (*Now, to Jack.*) I think I said this was a white hospital.

JACK (*Wearily.*) I know, lady . . . you told me.

NURSE. (*Her attention on the door.*) You don't have sense enough to do what you're told . . . you make trouble for yourself . . . you make trouble for other people.

JACK. (*Sighing.*) I don't care. . . .

NURSE. You'll care!

JACK. (*Softly, shaking his head.*) No . . . I won't care. (*Now, half to her, half to himself.*) We were driving along . . . not very fast . . . I don't think we were driving fast . . . we were in a hurry, yes . . . and I had been drinking . . . *we* had been drinking . . . but I *don't* think we were driving fast . . . not too fast . . .

NURSE. (*Her speeches now are soft comments on his.*) . . . driving drunk on the road . . . it not even dark yet . . .

74

JACK. . . . but then there was a car . . . I hadn't seen it . . . it couldn't have seen me . . . from a side road . . . hard, fast, sudden . . . (*Stiffens.*) . . . CRASH! (*Loosens.*) . . . and we weren't thrown . . . both of us . . . both cars stayed on the road . . . but we were stopped . . . my motor, running. . . . I turned it off . . . the door . . . the right door was all smashed in. . . . That's all it was . . . no more damage than that . . . but we had been riding along . . . laughing . . . it was cool driving, but it was warm out . . . and she had her arm out the window . . .

NURSE. . . . serves you right . . . drinking on the road . . .

JACK. . . . and I said . . . I said, Honey, we have crashed . . . you all right? (*His face contorts.*) And I looked . . . and the door was all pushed in . . . she was caught there . . . where the door had pushed in . . . her right side, crushed into the torn door, the door crushed into her right side. . . . BESSIE! BESSIE! . . . (*More to the Nurse, now.*) . . . but, ma'am . . . her arm . . . her right arm . . . was torn off . . . almost torn off from her shoulder . . . and there was blood . . . SHE WAS BLEEDING SO . . . !

NURSE. (*From a distance.*) Like water from a faucet . . . ? Oh, that is terrible . . . terrible. . . .

JACK. I didn't wait for nothin' . . . the other people . . . the other car . . . I started up . . . I started . . .

NURSE. (*More alert.*) You took *off*? . . . You took off from an accident?

JACK. Her arm, ma'am . . .

NURSE. You probably got police looking for you right now . . . you know that?

JACK. Yes, ma'am . . . I suppose so . . . and I drove . . . there was a hospital about a mile up . . .

NURSE. (*Snapping to attention.*) THERE! You went somewhere *else*? You been somewhere else already? What are you doing *here* with that woman then, hunh?

JACK. At the hospital . . . I came in to the desk and I told them what had happened . . . and they said, you sit down and wait . . . you go over there and sit down and wait a while. WAIT! It was a white hospital, ma'am . . .

NURSE. *This* is a white hospital, too.

JACK. I said . . . this is an emergency . . . there has been an accident. . . . YOU WAIT! You just sit down and wait. . . . I told them . . . I told them it was an emergency . . . I said . . . this woman is badly hurt. . . . YOU COOL YOUR HEELS! . . . I said, Ma'am, I got Bessie Smith out in that car there. . . . I DON'T CARE WHO YOU GOT OUT THERE, NIGGER . . . YOU COOL YOUR HEELS! . . . I couldn't wait there . . . her in the car . . . so I left there . . . I drove on . . . I stopped on the road and I was told where to come . . . and I came here.

NURSE. (*Numb, distant.*) I know who she is . . I heard her sing. (*Abruptly.*) You give me your name! You can't take off from an accident like that . . . I'll phone the police; I'll tell them where you are! (*The Intern and the Orderly re-enter, R. Their uniforms are bloodied. The Orderly moves stage-rear, avoiding Jack. The Intern moves in, staring at Jack.*) He drove away from an accident . . . he just took off . . . and he didn't come right here, either . . . he's been to one hospital *already.* I *warned* you not to get mixed up in this. . . .

INTERN. (*Softly.*) Shut up! (*Moves toward Jack, stops in front of him.*) You tell me something . . .

NURSE. I warned you! You didn't listen to me . . .

JACK. You want my name, too . . . is that what you want?

INTERN. No, that's not what I want. (*He is contained, but there is a violent emotion inside him.*) You tell me something. When you brought her here . . .

JACK. I brought her here. . . . They wouldn't help her. . . .

INTERN. All right. When you brought her here . . . when you brought this woman *here* . . .

NURSE. Oh, this is no plain woman . . . this is no ordinary nigger . . . this is Bessie Smith!

INTERN. When you brought this woman *here* . . . when you drove up *here* . . . when you brought this woman *here* . . . DID YOU KNOW SHE WAS DEAD? (*Pause.*)

NURSE. Dead! . . . This nigger brought a dead woman here?

INTERN. (*Afraid of the answer.*) Well . . . ?

NURSE. (*Distantly.*) Dead . . . dead.

JACK. (*Wearily, turning, moving toward the outside door, R.*) Yes . . . I knew she was dead. She died on the way here.

NURSE. (*Snapping to.*) Where you going? Where do you think you're going? I'm going to get the police here for you!

76

JACK. (*At the door.*) Just outside.

INTERN. (*As Jack exits.*) WHAT DID YOU EXPECT ME TO DO, EH? WHAT WAS I SUPPOSED TO DO? (*Jack pauses for a moment, looks at him blankly, closes the door behind him.*) TELL ME! WHAT WAS I SUPPOSED TO DO?

NURSE. (*Slyly.*) Maybe . . . maybe he thought you'd bring her back to life . . . great white doctor. (*Her laughter begins now, mounts to hysteria.*) Great . . . white . . . doctor. . . . Where are you going to go now . . . great . . . white . . . doctor? You are finished. You have had your last patient here. . . . Off you go, boy! You have had your last patient . . . a nigger . . . a dead nigger lady . . . WHO SINGS. Well . . . I sing, too, boy . . . I sing real good. You want to hear me sing? Hunh? You want to hear the way I sing? HUNH? (*Here she begins to sing and laugh at the same time. The singing is tuneless, almost keening, and the laughter is almost crying.*)

INTERN. (*Moves to her.*) Stop that! Stop that! (*But she can't. Finally he slaps her hard across the face. Silence. She is frozen, with her hand to her face where he hit her. He backs toward the* L. *door.*)

ORDERLY. (*His back to the wall.*) I never heard of such a thing . . . bringing a dead woman here like that. . . . I don't know what people can be thinking of sometimes. . . . (*The Intern exits,* L. *The room fades into silhouette again. . . . The great sunset blazes, music up.*)

## CURTAIN

# PROPERTY PLOT

## SCENE ONE

*On Stage*
Table
Chairs (2)
Glass of beer

*Off Stage*
Bottle of beer (Jack)
*Personal*
Dollar Bill (Bernie)

## SCENE TWO

*On Stage*
Wicker porch furniture, slightly
  worn

Cane (Father)

## SCENE FOUR

*On Stage*
Admissions desk and chair, at c.
Bench

Chairs (2)
Telephone

## SCENE FIVE

*On Stage*
Another admissions desk and
  chair, on raised platform

Telephone
*Off Stage*
Nail file (Second Nurse)

## SCENE SIX

*On Stage*
Clipboard, with papers—on desk,
  c.

*Personal*
Cigarettes and matches (Intern)

## SCENE EIGHT

*On Stage*
Letter opener, on desk, c.

*Off Stage*, L.
Pack of cigarettes (Orderly)
Containers of coffee (2) (Intern)

# Fam and Yam

An Imaginary Interview
(1960)

## THE PLAYERS

The Famous American Playwright (hereafter called FAM)—a no-longer thin gentleman, a year or so either side of fifty. What does he look like most? . . . a slightly rumpled account executive? . . . a faintly foppish Professor of History? Either one will do.

The Young American Playwright (hereafter called YAM)—an intense, bony young man, whose crew cut is in need of a trim; sweat socks, an over-long scarf, an old issue of *Evergreen Review* under one arm.

# Fam and Yam

## THE SCENE

*The living room of the East Side apartment of a famous American playwright, a view of the bridge, white walls, a plum-colored sofa, two Modiglianis, one Braque, a Motherwell and a Klein.*
*A Sunday afternoon.*
*At the beginning, Fam is alone, reading, on the plum-colored sofa, a decanter before him, a glass of sherry beside him. The door chime chimes, from the entrance hall, off-stage, L. Fam looks up, consults his wrist watch, frowns, puts down his book, drinks off his sherry, rises, moves off as the door chime chimes again. Maybe he clears his throat as he moves off. Sound of voices whence Fam vanished. . . . "Well, now, how do you do, sir." Fam re-enters, followed by Yam.*

FAM. (*Consulting his wrist watch again.*) Well, sir. Come in, come in.

YAM. (*Bounding behind him.*) I'm early; I apologize.

FAM. Are you? (*Consults his wrist watch again.*) Well, so you are. It doesn't matter, though. (*Indicating a chair beside the plum-colored sofa.*) Won't you . . . ?

YAM. (*With a quick glance at the paintings.*) Ah!

FAM. Hm?

YAM. It must be wonderful to throw away the reproductions!

FAM. The what?

YAM. Your paintings . . . it must be wonderful to throw away the . . .

FAM. Oh . . . yes. (*Indicating the chair again.*) Won't you . . . ?

YAM. Very nice place!

81

FAM. Uh . . . thank you. (*Indicating the chair again.*) Shall we . . . ?

YAM. I appreciate your seeing me; I really do.

FAM. Not at all; I was very happy. . . .

YAM. I hesitated writing you; I wasn't sure that . . . well, you know . . . I wasn't sure that I should; perhaps I shouldn't have.

FAM. (*Pause.*) Hm? . . . Oh! No, no; I was . . . uh . . . very pleased. (*Moves toward the plum-colored sofa.*) Perhaps if we . . .

YAM. (*At the window now.*) AH! And this;

FAM. (*Apprehensive.*) What?

YAM. This view!

FAM. (*Defensive.*) What . . . what about it?

YAM. Joan Crawford, Susan Hayward . . . everybody . . . !

FAM. (*Frightened.*) What?

YAM. (*Laughs.*) Oh, you know; all those movies they made . . . and they all had apartments over here, and they always had a view . . . just like this.

FAM. (*Pause.*) Um hum. I . . . uh . . . I have your letter here and (*looks around for the letter*) . . . I must say, it was most generous of you to . . .

YAM. (*As Fam discovers the letter in his pocket.*) Generous! No; not at all. It was the truth.

FAM. (*Smiling modestly, glancing at the letter.*) Oh, well, now . . . I . . . it does seem to me . . .

YAM. (*Moving in.*) No, it was the truth. You . . . along with a few others . . . Miller, Williams . . . Thornton Wilder, and . . . uh . . . (*Shrugs.*) . . . Inge . . . uh . . . you're . . . well, you're right up there.

FAM. (*Without much enthusiasm.*) You're very kind.

YAM. I think it's the continuum, really; that's so important.

FAM. The . . . uh . . . ?

YAM. The way you keep writing them . . . one after the other!

FAM. (*Smiling weakly, moving toward the sherry.*) Well, it's easier than writing them all at once. Ha, ha, ha.

YAM. (*Rushing on.*) I guess what I mean is: You're a real *pro.*

FAM. (*Considers it, then, proudly.*) Yes . . . Yes . . . I suppose you could say that.

YAM. Pro *is* the right word. What's-his-name . . . up at Columbia . . . you know who I mean . . . says that in his book *pro* is synonymous with high-class hack . . . but I don't agree with him there.

FAM. (*Offering the decanter.*) Drink?

YAM. No, thanks; I don't drink. . . .

FAM. (*Pouring himself another sherry.*) I do.

YAM. . . . this early. I suppose what what's-his-name really means is, that continued popular acceptance of a man's work, like yours. . . .

FAM. (*Too loud.*) What did you want to see me about . . . exactly? I couldn't quite tell from your letter . . . I mean, it was a very pleasant letter . . . very flattering . . . but, I'm still not clear. . . .

YAM. . . . but after all, you and a man like that just don't talk the same language.

FAM. (*Puzzled.*) Hm? . . . What? . . . Who?

YAM. What's-his-name . . . up at Columbia.

FAM. I . . .

YAM. What I came to see you about . . . maybe I didn't put it too well in my letter . . . is . . . well, I need your advice.

FAM. (*Softly, with becoming modesty.*) Well, I'd be happy . . . I don't know that I'm . . .

YAM. (*Plunging on.*) You see . . . I have to do an article on the theatre, and . . .

FAM. (*The corners of his mouth turning upward.*) You *have* to?

YAM. Well, I'm not *compelled* to . . . and it *is* on speculation. . . .

FAM. Ah, an *indefinite* article. . . . (*Chuckles.*)

YAM. And . . . uh . . . what? Oh! Yes . . . very good; very good, indeed.

FAM. (*Still chuckling.*) Words; words . . . they're such a pleasure.

YAM. At any rate, I *do* have to write this article. . . .

FAM. (*Businesslike . . . for fear of having offended.*) Yes; yes, by all means.

YAM. And I *would* appreciate your advice.

FAM. (*Knitting his brow.*) Certainly. (*Brightly.*) Oh, I've . . . I forgot to congratulate you on your . . . success . . . your . . . uh . . . off-Broadway play.

YAM. (*Pleased.*) Oh. . . .

FAM. Yes; yes, indeed . . . you must be very proud. It's called . . . uh . . .

YAM. DILEMMA, DERELICTION AND DEATH.

FAM. Uh . . . yes . . . yes, that's right . . . DILEMMA . . . DEATH. . . .

YAM. DILEMMA, DERELICTION AND DEATH.

FAM. Ah, yes . . . that's it. That's . . . that's quite a mouthful. It's down at the . . . uh . . .

YAM. East Third Street Playhouse.

FAM. Yes; yes. (*Pause.*) I must confess I haven't had a chance to . . . get down there yet. . . .

YAM. Oh, well, I . . .

FAM. Just opened, didn't it? And such good press!

YAM. Four months ago; yes.

FAM. Oh, my . . . that long! (*Pause.*) Well, time does . . . four months already . . . indeed!

YAM. (*Smiling eagerly.*) Yes!

FAM. (*Shooting his cuffs, aggressively cheerful.*) The new generation's knocking at the door. Gelber, Richardson, Kopit . . . (*Shrugs.*) . . . Albee . . . you. . . . (*Mock woe.*) You youngsters are going to push us out of the way. . . .

YAM. (*An unintentionally teeth-baring smile.*) Well, maybe there'll be room for all of us.

FAM. (*Rocking back.*) Uh . . . well . . . yes! (*Suspiciously.*) Let's hope so!

YAM. (*As Fam pours himself another sherry.*) Well, now . . . about the article.

FAM. (*Apprehensive.*) Ah . . . yes . . . that.

YAM. (*Moving in.*) It seemed to me best to start right off with a *bang!* (*Strikes a fist into the palm of the other hand. Fam jumps slightly.*) No pussy-footing around!

FAM. (*Backing off a little.*) No . . . yes; by all means.

YAM. A real attack . . . lay 'em all out . . . put it right on the line . . . and let 'em have it!

FAM. (*Eyeing Yam.*) Yes . . . well, we *do* need . . . uh . . . constructive critical journalism (*As his voice trails off.*) . . . if there is any such . . .

YAM. (*Breaking in.*) What I thought I'd do first . . . is make a list of villains . . . right at the beginning. You see, I'm going to call the piece "In Search of a Hero."

84

FAM. Well, I think that's . . .

YAM. Dandy, hunh? (*Chuckles* . . . *goes on.*) And so, I thought I'd make a list . . . right at the top. And list everybody!

FAM. Everybody?

YAM. Everybody! (*Plunging.*) And that's where you come in.

FAM. (*Looking toward the hall.*) I? . . . I'm not sure I . . .

YAM. That's where I need your help. You know these people . . . you've run up against them . . . you've . . . you've been exposed to the stupidity . . . the arrogance . . . the opportunism . . . the . . .

FAM. Well, I suppose I . . .

YAM. I know you have . . . I'm sure of it. Nobody could have gotten to the position you're in *without* coming in contact with it.

FAM. (*Cautiously, as he pours himself another sherry.*) Well, now . . . I've had a pretty easy time of it . . . I . . .

YAM. But you *have* run into it!

FAM. (*Wishing himself, or Yam, elsewhere.*) I *suppose* so . . . I . . .

YAM. Of course you have! So! Here's the list of villains. (*Paces. Counts on his fingers.*) The theatre owners . . . the producers . . . the backers . . . the theatre parties . . . the unions . . . the critics . . . the directors . . . and the playwrights themselves. . . . That's the list. (*Smiles.*)

FAM. (*Overwhelmed.*) That . . . that doesn't . . . (*A weak smile.*) that doesn't leave much room for a hero, does it?

YAM. (*Jumping on it.*) That's just the point! Everybody's culpable.

FAM. Oh, my.

YAM. I hope you'll talk frankly.

FAM. Well . . . certainly. . . .

YAM. Because, I don't want to go off half-cocked. . . .

FAM. (*Moving toward the sherry decanter again.*) Well, I'm sure none of us does. Are you sure you don't . . . you wouldn't like a drink?

YAM. No . . . no, thank you. But you . . . you keep right on.

FAM. (*Pauses . . . irritated.*) Thank you . . . I will.

YAM. (*Ignoring Fam's tone.*) Now, for the theatre owners. . . . I thought one might call them something like . . . ignorant, greedy, hit-happy real estate owners.

FAM. (*Shocked . . . amused.*) Oh . . . oh, my . . . that is strong, isn't it?

YAM. And then, the producers. . . . How about: opportunistic, out-for-a-buck businessmen, masquerading as . . .

FAM. Oh, yes . . . wonderful . . . wonderful . . . very strong. Oh my!

YAM. You get the idea?

FAM. (*Pouring himself another sherry. He is pacing, now, the decanter in one hand, the glass in the other.*) Yes . . . yes, I do. That's . . . that's really laying it on the line. (*Chuckles.*)

YAM. And I thought it would be good to say that most of our playwrights are nothing better than businessmen themselves . . . you know . . . out for the loot . . . just as cynically as anyone else. . . .

FAM. (*A little tipsy by now.*) Oh, ho ho ho ho!

YAM. . . . and that our directors are slick, sleight-of-hand artists . . . talking all noble and uncompromising *until* they get into rehearsal . . . and *then* . . .

FAM. (*Doubled over with mirth.*) Yes . . . yes! Ha ha ha ha!

YAM. . . . and about the critics . . . how they've set themselves up as sociological arbiters . . . misusing their function . . . and . . .

FAM. (*Wildly amused . . . encouraging.*) Yes . . . yes . . . go on . . . go on!

YAM. . . . and then tacking into the agencies . . . call them assembly lines or something . . .

FAM. Ha ha ha ha!

YAM. . . . and then the pin-heads . . .

FAM. (*Beside himself.*) The pin-heads! Hee hee hee . . . who are they?

YAM. (*Modestly.*) Oh, the theatre parties. . . .

FAM. The theatre parties. (*Laughs uncontrollably . . . knocks over an occasional table.*) Boy! Give it to 'em, eh? . . . Lay it right on the line! . . . Let 'em all have it! . . . Ha ha ha ha. . . . Mow 'em down!

YAM. (*Beaming.*) You like it? You like the idea!

FAM. Like it! I love it! Hee hee hee hee! It's the funniest thing I've ever heard!

YAM. (*Very serious.*) I'm glad.

FAM. C'mon . . . have a drink. Heh heh heh.

YAM. No . . . no . . . I must go. . . . I've taken up too much of your time already.

FAM. OH, no . . . it's early. C'mon . . . stick around. Ha ha ha ha.

YAM. (*Extending his hand, which is not taken, Fam's hands being full.*) No . . . no, really, sir . . . I must go. Thank you very much . . . very much indeed.

FAM. Ho ho ho . . . don't mention it. Oh, my . . . I haven't laughed so much. . . . (*They both move into the entrance hall. From there . . . goodbyes—thank you's . . . don't mention its. Sound of door closing. Fam re-enters, walks about, pours himself another sherry.*) Ha ha ha ha. The pin-heads! Hee hee hee hee! Oh, my . . . oh my. (*Shakes his head . . . puts the decanter and glass down, moves to right the fallen table . . . does so.*) The pin-heads! Ha ha ha ha! (*Roams around the room, giggling, laughing. The telephone rings. He moves to it.*) Heh heh heh. Hello . . . ?

YAM'S VOICE. (*Loud—over a speaker.*) Uh . . . hello there . . . it's me again.

FAM. Oh . . . you. . . . C'mon back up an' have a drink.

YAM'S VOICE. Oh no . . . no. . . . I just wanted to thank you again. I'm just downstairs . . . and I wanted to thank you again.

FAM. Don't mention it, my boy! Thank *you.* Ha ha ha ha!

YAM'S VOICE. Thank you very much for the interview. Thank you sir.

FAM. You're welcome . . . you're welcome . . . heh heh heh. (*He hangs up . . . strolls.*) You're welcome . . . you're welcome. (*Suddenly stops.*) THE INTERVIEW!!! THE INTERVIEW!!!!! (*His face turns ashen . . . his mouth drops open. One of the Modiglianis frowns . . . the Braque peels . . . the Klein tilts . . . and the Motherwell crashes to the floor.*)

## CURTAIN

## PROPERTY PLOT

*On Stage*
Plum colored sofa
Modern paintings:
    2 Modiglianis
    1 Braque
    1 Motherwell
    1 Klein
Tables and chairs—in clean-lined, modern style
Decanter of sherry
Wine glasses (2)
Book
Telephone

*Personal*
Wristwatch (Fam)
Letter, in pocket (Fam)

*Off* L.
Sweat socks (Yam)
Over-long scarf (Yam)
Copy of *Evergreen Review* **(Yam)**